Understand Your Dreams

Understand Your Dreams
1500 Basic Dream Images
and
How to Interpret Them

Alice Anne Parker

H J KRAMER INC
Tiburon, California

H J Kramer Inc
P.O. Box 1082
Tiburon, CA 94920

Editor: Nancy Grimley Carleton
Editorial Assistant: Claudette Charbonneau
Cover Art: *Wormhole* © 1993 by Hal Kramer
Cover Design: Jim Marin/Marin Graphic Services
Typesetting: Classic Typography
Book Production: Schuettge & Carleton
Manufactured in the United States of America.
10 9 8 7 6 5 4

Library of Congress Cataloging-in-Publication Data:
Parker, Alice Anne, 1939–
    Understand your dreams : 1500 basic dream images and how to
interpret them / Alice Anne Parker.
        p. cm.
    ISBN 0–915811–59–6 : $12.00
    1. Dreams. 2. Imagery (Psychology) I. Title.
BF10814.P37 1991, 1995
135'.3—dc20   90–50862
                                                                  CIP

With heartfelt thanks to:
Dr. Thomas Maughan
Jane Roberts
Eya Yellin
Alvan Perry Parker

To Our Readers

The books we publish are our
contribution to an emerging world based
on cooperation rather than on competition, on
affirmation of the human spirit rather than on self-
doubt, and on the certainty that all humanity is
connected. Our goal is to touch as many
lives as possible with a message
of hope for a better world.

Hal and Linda Kramer,
Publishers

. . . For true symbols have something illimitable about them. They are inexhaustible in their suggestive and instructive power. . . . The meanings have to be constantly reread, understood afresh. And it is anything but an orderly work – this affair of interpreting the always unpredicted and astonishing metamorphoses. No systematist who greatly valued his reputation would willingly throw himself open to the risk of the adventure. It must, therefore, remain to the reckless dilettante. Hence the following book.

Heinrich Zimmer,
The King and the Corpse,
edited by Joseph Campbell

Contents

Introduction to Second Edition

I want to thank all of the readers who have mailed me lists of images to include in the second edition of *Understand Your Dreams.* I especially want to thank all of you who wrote to say how much you liked the book or how useful it was to you! These letters and notes always seem to arrive at the exact moment I need a bit of praise or support, and they are much appreciated.

Like many of you, I have had the experience of looking up a dream image in the book, reading the associations or the questions listed, and then thinking with a bit of irritation, "No, that's not it at all." Usually this happens when the image means something specific to me or to the particular dream. However, even when the personal meaning of the image is far removed from the associations and questions listed, reading them always helps to reveal deeper levels of meaning for me.

Please remember, the key to dream interpretation is always feeling. How did you feel in the dream? How did you feel about the particular object, person, or activity? To one dreamer, a "banquet" might be a boring ritual; to another, it could mean long sought-after acknowledgment. "Formal celebration" and "recognition," the associations listed in the book, would have different significance for each dreamer. Yet, once the feeling has been identified, the appropriate meaning can unfold.

I am also grateful to Sam Wagonvoord and Ted Sax at Radio Station K108 in Honolulu, to John Kelleher and the brilliantly creative Gray Gleeson at Station KGU, also in Honolulu, and especially to all who have called in their dream images to "Dreamline," my call-in radio show on dreams.

Finally, I want to thank friends who have called or written to me to make sure items were included in this edition, especially Wendy Saito, Kristina Natalie, Luana Kuhns, Laura Paulson, Jesse Molina, Karma Blank, and my colleague, Toni Gallardi. My husband, Henry Holthaus, deserves all praise for his notes from the "Dreamline" radio show, and for his unflagging good humor. I am especially grateful to Nancy Grimley Carleton for her patience and fine editorial touch and to Uma Ergil at H J Kramer, for her generous support of my writing and for the beautiful work she has done on this edition.

Acknowledgments

Several years ago, my friend Bosco d'Bruzzi suggested that I write a book on dream images. Like most serious dream workers, I had a powerful aversion to the idea of a dream dictionary, even though I owned a collection of fascinating versions of nineteenth-century best-sellers, including *What Your Dream Meant* by Martini the Palmist.

Then one day as I was leafing through *Heal Your Body*, Louise Hay's invaluable handbook on the metaphysical sources for physical problems, I realized that a comparable book on dream images would be an effective tool for anyone interested in dreams. My friend Sara Halprin suggested that I offer "associations" for the images rather than "meanings," and the book was on its way.

I particularly want to thank Louise Hay for inspiring the design of this book, and for her visionary, yet matter-of-fact, guidance.

I am also indebted to Gabrielle Lusser Rico and Tony Buzan, who independently developed similar techniques of clustering, or arranging information in a pattern of circles, as I have done with dreams. Rico developed this process of nonlinear brainstorming as a means of stimulating creativity and coherence in student writers in the United States. At the same time, in England, Tony Buzan used a process he called "mapping" as a way of accessing both sides of the brain while organizing a mass of information. I have long used Tony's mapping technique, as described in his book *Use Both Sides of Your Brain,* to play with ideas and organize workshop material, but it wasn't until I read Rico's *Writing the Natural Way* that I saw how useful the clustering process could be for recording dreams.

Each of us is honored by constant friends who support and encourage us through the disappointments that lead to our success. I am privileged to include in this category Tam Mossman, whose expert advice has contributed enormously to my confidence and growth as a writer. My dear friend LaUna Huffines gracefully led me to the perfect publishers, Hal and Linda Kramer. My daughter, April Severson, my husband,

Henry Holthaus, and my allies, Freude Bartlett and Mary Kathryn Cope, receive my heartfelt thanks for their years of relentless confidence in my work. This book owes a vast, if unspecifiable, debt to the friendship of Mel Lee, Lana Sawyer, Owen Sawyer, Barbara Such, Peter Bloch, Mary Platt, Kathy Vinton, Herb Long, Harold Cope, Terence Stamp, Sheila Rainer, Pamela Norris, Peggy Donavan, and Herb Goodman. I am also grateful to the members of my Honolulu workshop in Interactive Dreaming, who gave me such useful feedback while I was developing the image catalogue. Thanks to Sandra Brockman, Mary Kathryn Cope, Nancy Crane, Bosco d'Bruzzi, Carla Hayashi, Henry Holthaus, Jan Kaeo, Luana Kuhns, Patricia Martin, Garrett Miyake, Karen Miyake, Georgia Putnam, Jessica Putnam, Doris Rarick, Helen Schlapak, John Squires, and Margaret Stallings.

My thanks also go to all of those who have so generously shared their dreams in my workshops, on "Dreamline," my radio show, and in the "Dreamline" newspaper column.

Part One
Remembering and Understanding Your Dreams

Dream Work

Over the past thirty-eight years, I've worked with thousands of dreams—my own as well as other people's. And after talking with scores of clients, I've concluded that there are three basic barriers to satisfying dream work.

The first barrier is obvious and all too familiar: *not being able to remember dreams in the first place.* If this is a problem for you, begin by writing down any dream—or dream fragment—that you remember, from any time in your life. Follow the basic steps for processing dreams that I will outline in the next few pages. The simple act of paying close attention to a dream, even one from your distant past, is often enough to stimulate a new pattern of increasing dream recall.

But what if you can't *ever* remember any dream? There is still hope! Instead of recording a dream, record one of your early memories as if it were a dream. Start by recalling a childhood memory—if possible, choose one that resonates with strong emotions—but even a dimly remembered early event will do. Just one or two images, plus the feelings associated with them, will give you plenty to work with. Then, by processing this memory using the basic techniques that follow, you can open a door to the fascinating (and sometimes very practical) messages waiting just across the threshold of your waking consciousness. In most cases, once you have given careful attention to a dream or dreamlike memory, you'll find yourself recalling dreams on a more regular basis.

Now for the second and most common barrier to dream work: *not being able to understand the dreams you do remember.* In this section, I'll be providing you with some basic tools for unfolding the many levels of meaning that most dreams offer you. The index in the second part of this book will give you a head start on making sense of even the most impenetrable dream symbols.

The third barrier to dream work may be the most serious of all: *most of us simply don't have enough time to record our dreams.* No matter how dedicated you are, the pressure of getting kids off to school, the interruption of morning phone calls, and all the demands of your daily rush are there to interfere. With even a few minutes of delay, vital details of a dream can simply evaporate. One of my clients complained of leaving her dream notebook on a corner dresser instead of conveniently close to her bed. By the time she crossed the room, it was too late—the entire dream had faded from her memory.

How can you hope to make sense of what you can no longer remember? Even if you catch your dreams and remember them well, you still need some effective—and *fast*—way of getting them down before they slip away. The following eight-step process will help you both remember *and* understand your dreams.

An Eight-Step Process for Understanding Your Dreams

Step 1: Record the
Images of Your Dream.

Dreams often have a funny way of happening all at once. They don't occur in a linear, one-two-three sequence, as do events in waking life. Writing them down in narrative paragraphs not only takes too long, but it often violates the sense of the original dream in which events relate and interconnect in a much more circular, holistic, and organic form. So rather than write your dream down, try dropping dream images into an easy-to-draw pattern of circles.

This takes much less time than the usual way of writing out a dream one sentence at a time, and also allows you to relate dream events to each other in a more flowing and flexible form. Just drop the dream's main images into a pattern of circles and then let the information cook while you get on with your day. For each element, draw a circle large enough to express the importance of each image or event. Use one big circle to "enclose" a few words that describe the central action, perhaps with smaller surrounding circles to represent the sequence of events. Don't feel it's necessary to duplicate the perfect circles of the following patterns. Quickly sketch a rough circle and jot down the basic images. See Figure 1 for some examples of possible patterns.

With this technique, you can quickly record all of the dream's main components—more than enough to jog your memory later, when you have time to review the diagram. This method is not only faster than writing out a dream in complete sentences, but also gives you a more accurate record of the original experience. The "splash pattern" diagram allows you to relate dream events to one another in a more flowing and flexible form.

It may take a few mornings for you to become completely comfortable with this new system, but it will allow you to record

Figure 1: Sample Patterns
for Dream Circles

evolving dream event

setting
or
central action of dream

evolving dream events

related but independent images

You may wish to connect the circles with arrows or symbols.

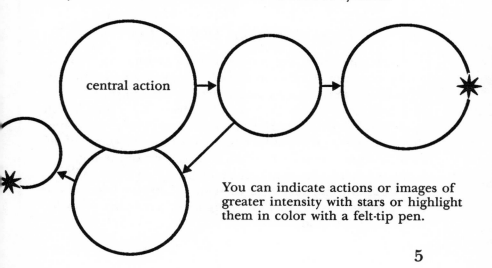

central action

You can indicate actions or images of
greater intensity with stars or highlight
them in color with a felt-tip pen.

even long and complex dreams quickly, even when you are particularly rushed.

Step 2: What Word or Phrase Best Expresses Your Feeling in This Dream?

You can tackle Step 2 as you are driving to work or sitting quietly with a second cup of coffee in the morning, or in the evening before you go to bed. Ask yourself, "How did I feel in my dream?" or "How did the dream make me feel?"

The answer should be easy, if sometimes a bit ambiguous: "curious," "worried," and "confused" are common replies. With a bad dream, the answer may be "anxious," or even "terrified." An ecstatic dream may produce a "blissful" feeling; my own very favorite dreams leave me with a feeling that everything is just fine, that things are all coming together perfectly.

Often, though, the answer you give yourself will be a bit more complex, as in "I wonder why I haven't lived in all these beautiful rooms!" Or "I can't figure out how to get my bags packed in time and I'm afraid I'll miss the flight!" Here, your clues lie in the emotionally evocative words: *"I wonder why I haven't lived . . . ," "I can't figure out . . . ,"* and *"I'm afraid I'll miss . . . "*

Step 3: When Is This Same Feeling Present in Your Waking Life?

Tracking down the source of each feeling can be a bit tricky, but in most cases you will feel an immediate tingle of recognition, and some particular area or issue in your life will leap into focus. Using the examples given under Step 2, you might discover that you haven't lived out your childhood dreams, that you can't figure out how to pack all the "baggage" of accumulated attitudes and beliefs and still "make the flight" to a greater awareness of what's really going on in your life.

By asking and answering these questions, you begin to use the valuable insights that every night's dreams offer you with such inventive guidance.

6

Step 4: What Were the Significant Activities in Your Dream?

List the key activities in your dream, and turn to Part Two. For each action, look up the associations given in the second column and the questions in the third column. If the associations and questions seem appropriate, write your answers down, especially if you've been dreaming about the same activities over a considerable period of time.

At first, some of these "typical" dream activities may be hard for you to pinpoint. Many of us have regular dream patterns that have become so familiar that we may take them completely for granted. For example, do you always find yourself hunting for a new apartment, fighting the enemy, going shopping, finding bills and coins, or trying to get a decent meal? I have been traveling in my dreams for my entire life. This activity seemed so natural and ordinary that I never examined the meaning behind it. Instead, I usually focused my attention on the method of traveling and the inevitable delays and problems en route, completely failing to notice that the essential framework of my dreams was so often a journey. It was a real breakthrough when I finally noticed that these dreams were giving me pithy bulletins on my personal *bildungsroman,* my inner search for the best routes and the most direct passage to my goal of greater consciousness. I continue to be on the road in many of my dreams, but now I'm more alert to the deeper meaning of these regular travel updates!

So consider the activities of your dream, particularly if they are familiar to you from many previous recurrent dreams. Look up these activities in Part Two of this book and see if the associations given seem appropriate to you. Sometimes these associations may not fit for you, but often just seeing what *isn't* perfectly accurate will stimulate you to come up with a more exact answer. Then ask yourself the question or questions that appear in the right-hand column. Again, even if these questions don't quite fit, they will usually give you a clue to the question you *do* need to ask.

Working With a Partner

Active dreaming is a lot more fun if you have someone you can use as a sounding board. Sometimes simply having someone else ask you the questions in the right-hand column of Part Two will help stimulate an answer. Sharing a dream dialogue with your partner or mate, with other family members, or with a good friend enriches everyone's dreams and the collective awareness as well. Remember that increased consciousness is highly contagious.

Step 5: List the Characters in Your Dream. What Part of You Does Each Dream Figure Represent?

For Step 5, list the "cast" of your dream—the figures and characters who appeared in it—and examine them one by one. If they are real people known to you personally, they may represent themselves or your feelings about them: your wife is really your wife, your friend your friend, and so on. In unfolding the dream's meaning, however, you will find it useful to describe these familiar persons with a word or two: "My wife is *capable* and *extravagant.*" "My friend is *weak willed* but *well intentioned.*"

Now, a slightly tougher assignment: ask what *aspects* of yourself are reflected by these various dream figures. In other words, in what ways are *you* being capable and extravagant? How are *you* judging yourself as weak willed but well intentioned? Also, look up Wife and Friend to see what general associations those relationships may present for you.

When apparent strangers play a part in your dream script, you can look up their roles or professions in Part Two. For Dentist, for example, the given association is "work on independence and power." If these associations feel appropriate to you, then ask the questions listed for each character; for Dentist, the question is "What part of me needs strengthening?"

8

Step 6: List the Significant Places, Objects, Colors, and Events in the Dream.

Once again, if the associations and questions listed feel relevant to your dream, write down your answer.

If your dream dentist in Step 5 was working on your teeth, you will find for Teeth the further associations of "independence, power, ability to nourish and communicate." Here, the questions to ask yourself are "Where in my life do I fear dependence?" and "What do I wish to say?"

List all the objects, places, colors, and events of your dream—especially ones that seem particularly vivid or noticeably unusual or out of place. In most dreams, certain places and objects will be prominent. When you remember the dream later, they will stand out with greater detail, or else you will sense a stronger emotional field around them. When you look up their associations and the questions to ask yourself, pay particular attention to these stronger images.

The associations given in Part Two are usually neutral or positive. If you dream about an angry dog, for example, you will find Dog associated with the positive qualities of loyalty and trustworthiness. If your dream dog seemed threatening to you, adjust the questions accordingly. Ask yourself, "Where do I feel *threatened* by lack of loyalty?" or "What do I *not* trust in myself?"

The list of images presented here cannot be exhaustive, of course. Anything you can imagine (and many things you haven't imagined!) will turn up in dreams. But, to track down the meanings and associations of these images, you can use related objects or ideas as clues. For example, if you dream that your teeth are falling out, you may be distressed to find that there is no listing for that exact image. But looking up both Teeth and Falling will lead you to the exciting questions "Where in my life do I fear dependence?" and "Where do I want to land?"

Perhaps, for you, fear of dependence has been a hurdle to intimate relationships, making you afraid to fall in love. Yet with this dream's help, you might discover that you really want to "land" in the kind of supportive and trusting relationship you have always longed for.

Personal Dream Vocabularies

Most of us have expanded dream vocabularies based on the interests and specialties of our waking life. In one of my dream workshops, an interior designer regularly reported dreams with richly detailed images featuring elaborate patterns and textures. To understand these dreams, she began by working with the primary associations for images such as walls, carpet, furniture, chair, antiques, colors, and so on. To follow the more subtle levels of meaning, however, she had to take the further step of asking herself what she felt about each image's specific details.

One of the interior designer's dreams featured two chairs; the first she described as an original Louis XV side chair upholstered in lovat green silk jacquard. The chair was beautiful and valuable, but also stiff, fragile, and quite uncomfortable; this, she concluded, represented her discomfort with old principles and attitudes. The second chair, a copy from a later historical period, was less valuable, but much more useful.

She then considered each specific detail, seeking more personal levels of meaning. It was an education in style to hear her examine the precise significance of Louis XV versus Directoire, of lovat green versus viridian, of jacquard weave versus petit point. As she pursued each detail of these designs, more and more information unfolded about changes she was preparing to make—both professionally and personally.

When you work with rich imagery derived from your own areas of interest, ask yourself how you feel about the particular details in the dream that have caught your attention. Personal levels of association will quickly expand the general meanings and questions provided in Part Two of this book.

Sample Dream Analysis

Here's an example of steps 1 through 6, taken from my own dream journal. The dream story was brief, but significant. First, let me report the dream in conventional linear form:

10

I am driving in a car with my old friend Joan. We are cutting class together to go swimming. I am feeling very pleased to have this time with her. Then I am leaving my daughter April at the train station. I feel a bit worried about her having all of the details of her journey together and making her connection to the boat on time.

I am uncertain which part of the dream happened first.

Using the circle technique of Step 1, I could easily and rapidly fit these two events or images into two large circles, thus:

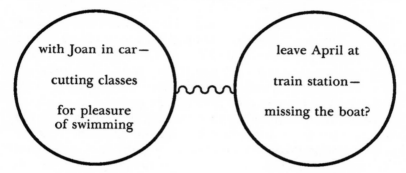

Since I wasn't sure which part of the dream happened first, I drew an odd wiggly line between the two circles. The activities seemed to offer different choices of behavior—as if one balanced, or excluded, the other.

Now for Step 2: What word or phrase best expresses your feeling in this dream? First I wrote the phrase "missing the boat!" That was my strongest feeling. I had awakened with the familiar sense of excitement, coupled with that special anxiety that ship's whistles or train timetables can provoke in me. "Will we make it on time?" Then I also wrote: "*Worried* that I don't stay with April—but *pleased* to spend time with Joan."

Step 3: When is this same feeling present in your waking life? Ouch! No tingle of recognition for me. As soon as I thought about these emotions, the sensation was more like a nasty twinge in the back of my neck. "With regard to work and ambition," I wrote, "I am worried that I will miss the 'boat' of success—yet also, I believe that I already know what I need to know and that I can 'cut classes' to give time to old friends."

11

I noticed that in my journal I skipped Step 4, the question about identifying significant dream activities—but I'll return to that later. Now, Step 5: What part of you does each dream figure represent? I started by considering the characteristics of my daughter April, who was then a student at a prestigious university. She seemed to represent fulfillment of ambition to me. I also added that she knew how to enjoy herself and that I felt a deep and abiding love for her. Translating this information I saw that she embodied—or reflected—these traits for me.

For Joan, I wrote, "failure of ambition," "pleasure denying," and "betrayal of friendship." That is, I saw her as someone who had not fulfilled her early ambitions, who had denied herself many pleasures, and who had betrayed our friendship. I realized that she represented the part of me that feels like a failure, denies joy, and withholds love. Not a pretty picture!

After you have worked through the relevant associations and questions prompted by your dreams, you will have a good idea of what areas and issues in your life are clamoring for transformation. Now, instead of remaining the passive observer of events, you can become an active participant in your dream creation.

Step 7: What Changes, If Any, Would You Like to Make in This Dream?

Even a bad dream is a stimulus for change, pointing out where you are ready to grow. Simply because a bad dream *is* so powerful, it forcefully draws your attention to whatever area of your life is ready for work. A nightmare—about teeth falling out, for example—may be pointing the way to a joyous, committed partnership. Just recognizing that fact is a step in the right direction.

And, then, *decide what changes, if any, you would like to make in the dream.* Each and every element of your dream belongs to you. You can change it as you wish, and you will benefit directly and dramatically from the energy you release by doing so. It is almost always easier to make the change in a dream *before* you attempt a similar transformation in your waking life.

Once you do so, you can trust that similar changes will begin to appear in your waking life.

Begin by imagining different endings to your dream, particularly if it is part of a pattern or series that has been cropping up again and again for any length of time. Rewriting your dream script is not mere wishful thinking. When you play around with alternative solutions, you are using what is sometimes called "lateral thinking"—creative, playful manipulation of the images generated by the deepest levels of your own consciousness to resolve what are often lifelong issues and limitations.

When you find a really satisfying solution to a longtime dream problem, review your new plan as you are falling to sleep. If, like me, you find yourself constantly traveling around, enduring the hassles of too-tight schedules and missing suitcases, then maybe it's time you chartered your own plane! In your imagination, declare that your flight will leave when *you* are ready, baggage and all, and not before. You'll even have time to go back for the red suitcase that fell out of the back of the car as you were racing to the airport.

Start by rerunning your dream in one of its familiar forms, but then graft the new ending in place. When you go to sleep, expect the dream to reappear with some surprising new twists, but now you are ready to resolve it with new solutions or a creative alternative—and be confident that you will wake up with a great feeling of success.

Going back to the previous example from my dream journal, I resolved to make a conscious change in that rather unsettling dream. What changes would I like to make in this dream? What parts of it did I enjoy? I wrote, "I would like to stay at the train station until April is aboard the train, thus guaranteeing that she will not miss the boat. I enjoyed the other part of the dream, knowing it was okay to take time away from studies to swim and talk with Joan. I felt we could rebuild our lost friendship."

Changing Bad Dreams Into Good Ones

Several years ago, I worked with a woman who related a classic recurrent nightmare. In her dream, she would awaken to hear someone entering her house. All the appropriate creaks would sound, and she would hear slow, heavy footsteps coming down the hallway toward her bedroom. Frozen with terror, she would be unable to call to her roommates for help. As the door slowly swung open in the dream, she would awaken for real—to find herself in bed, trembling with fear.

In my client's first breakthrough with this dream, she found herself on a sailboat, watching her recurrent nightmare unfold on the screen of a television set. At first, she identified with the horror movie and was enormously frightened. But then, realizing that it was only a show on TV, she walked up to the set and changed the channel.

The dream had terrorized my client for years, and she dreaded its appearance. It was understandably difficult for her to approach it as an opportunity—to anticipate it and be ready to change it. I was very pleased to see her reverse this pattern: by watching the event take place on a TV screen, she was distancing herself from the fear and was genuinely prepared to "turn the old story off."

After this, however, my client experienced several very frightening dreams that escalated in terror. She also had a lurking fear that the dream was precognitive, warning of some event that would eventually take place in her waking life. The dream pattern escalated to incorporate this fear, so that she found herself waking into the dream, each time believing that it was actually happening.

My client regularly practiced visualizing different endings to the dream, replaying the new script until she felt at ease with a conclusion. All of her first solutions involved successfully calling out and having help actually arrive. In one early variation, it was a kitten who came to rescue her—that is, she was assisted by an aspect of the self that was feminine and cuddly, yet fiercely independent and able to care for itself. This solution made it clear that she was on her way to releasing and transforming the dream.

I have telescoped a longer sequence of dreams into these few examples. The process actually took place over a period of many months and included a number of variations on this basic theme. In the final stage of transformation, my client's

14

dream reverted to its usual pattern. This time, as the door swung slowly open, she remained asleep and determined to see *what* was so frightening. It was a hairy monster. She looked at him carefully and concluded that he led a joyless life. Then she arose from her bed and invited him to waltz! The hairy monster was delighted to accept, and the bad dream melted away.

The invitation to dance seemed a brilliant resolution, and I was most impressed with my client's courageous struggle with her personal dream nemesis. She did say the hairy monster was not too light on his feet and annoyed her by stepping on her toes.

The general theme of this client's dream is actually a fairly common one. In her particular version, a hairy monster was the villain, although other clients of mine have encountered the frying pan man, the hot dog man, the balloon man, the homicidal maniac, and the Ku Klux Klan samurai. (The negative aspect of the self has many faces!)

Step 8: Briefly Summarize the Dream's Meaning. How Does This Apply to Your Waking Life?

In order to anchor and solidify successful dream transformations, it is useful to answer the question "How does this dream apply to my waking life today?" The energy released with dream resolution can trigger concurrent breakthroughs in waking life: perhaps a new relationship will blossom, or you'll find greater satisfaction in work. A successful pregnancy, or even the end of a troubling marriage can result.

In my dream of Joan and my daughter April, I asked myself that same question: "How does this apply to my waking life?" I wrote, "I'm afraid that I am taking time to deal with what is important but secondary, while denying myself the time to care for what is of deepest value for me. I fear that this pattern will make me miss the boat of fulfillment."

The last thing I did was to draw in my journal two new sets of circles. Into them, I dropped the constellation of opposing traits that I observed in the two characters in my dream. The diagram looked like this:

J: witty, self-denying, self-defeating, obsessed by physical beauty, hungry for relationship

A: witty, fulfilling new ambition, self-respecting, successful, interested in physical beauty, working on relationship

problematic   lovable

This step is an extension of the usual process. I used it to understand better what parts of myself were at issue in the dream. I then labeled one constellation of traits "problematic" and the other one "lovable."

My efforts at changing this dream were followed by a series of new dreams in which I was exploring and evaluating new living spaces. Looking up Apartment and House under images, I found the questions "What part of myself do I occupy?" and "What do I believe or fear about myself?"

Since Joan was often with me in my dreams, as I considered whether the house or apartment would do, I concluded that I was missing something about her that continued to be important and that I was actively working on in myself. What might her greatest problem be? The answer came immediately: Joan did not love or accept herself. This self-judgment she then projected to the world at large, with a terrible effect on her relationships with others—including the men in her life, family, and friends like me.

I concluded that by exploring new living spaces with a self-judging aspect of myself, I was giving time and attention to a part of me that I had ignored and possibly denied. With this understanding, the figure of Joan disappeared from my dreams.

16

April continues to be a regular member of my personal cast, usually appearing in dreams in which I am examining professional choices.

Finally I went back to the issue of dream activities, which I had so conveniently skipped when I was first working with the dream in my journal. I was "swimming" with Joan, but was afraid of "missing the boat" that April was heading for. Swimming is associated with freedom and joy of movement in the water—the area of the unconscious and of emotion.

A boat allows safe and rapid travel over water. I concluded that it was relatively easy for me to take the time to explore the unconscious joyously. For example, working with my own and others' dreams is a great pleasure for me! More pleasure than work, in fact.

However, I was concerned about "missing" a more conventional means of travel. Some of my fears about not being successful must reflect my reluctance to go places by orthodox means. This connected with my daughter April, who has decided to follow a conventional mode of success by returning to college. I reassured myself that I can always dive off the boat for a refreshing dip in the sea of dreams!

Case History Using the Eight-Step Process

To review how to use the eight-step process for understanding your own dreams, I'd like to present a final case history: a vivid and meaningful dream experienced by a forty-three-year-old businessman who attended one of my Honolulu workshops in Interactive Dreaming. After processing the dream, he felt he achieved a significant personal breakthrough.

First I will quote his verbal report of the dream as he presented it during our workshop:

I am walking past the back door of my parents' house, where I grew up.

I look out the window, but see my reflection instead. I notice that I have an enormous erection and I'm nude. I look down at myself and see that I do have an erection, but it is nowhere near the size of the reflected penis.

I look back at the window thinking that it must be the type of glass that is making my penis look so big.

Now let me quote his written work on the dream as it appeared in his journal, with only minor editorial changes. His journal entry, using circles to diagram the dream, looked like this:

1. Record the images of your dream.

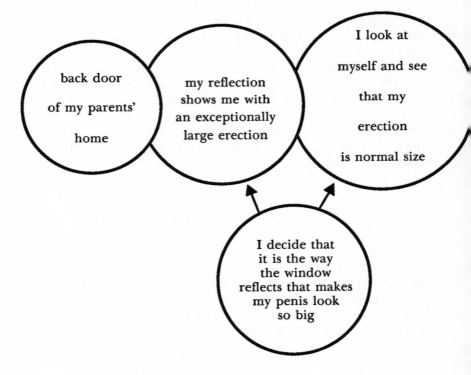

2. What word or phrase best expresses your feeling in this dream?

I am interested in the effect of looking bigger and more impressive produced by the back door window.

3. When is this same feeling present in your waking life?

In my awake life I have a similar feeling when the world perceives me as a successful businessman.

4. What were the significant activities in your dream?

I was observing myself, and, particularly, the "size" of my masculine attributes!

5. List the characters in your dream. What part of you does each dream figure represent?

Just me . . . representing me!

6. List the significant places, objects, colors, and events in the dream.

My parents' house = the parental attitudes, beliefs, fears, and also the beliefs I grew up with and still hold unconsciously.

My erection = creative power. What do I want to do or make? I do want to make a "big" success of my business. I want to feel as successful as the outside world believes me to be.

Nude = Where in my life am I ready to be seen? I am ready to see myself as successful.

Back = Unconscious, "back there," what I can't see. I don't consciously agree with my parents, but the fears and beliefs are still back there.

The back door is a passage out with a window that lets me view where it leads. I get a reflection as in a mirror, which makes me ask: What am I ready to see? I'm ready to see myself as successful, which would be a passage out of my parents' beliefs about limitations and success.

7. What changes, if any, would you like to make in this dream?

I would like to walk through the door and participate in the larger world's view of me.

8. Briefly summarize the dream's meaning. How does this apply to your waking life?

This dream is about the limitations of my beliefs, particularly unconscious beliefs about success in the world. As long as I continue to hold my parents' point of view, my power will remain relatively modest, even though the reflection from outside (that is, from the world) is much larger.

This dream didn't feel very sexual, although I think my parents' attitudes about being careful – not "exposing" yourself, never taking chances – also apply to sexuality.

As long as I am in my parents' house (of limited ideas, ambitions, and beliefs about personal power), I won't really own the power that the outside world already reflects as belonging to me.

In his dream, this businessman felt he had successfully "uncovered" feelings that had been limiting his *experience* of professional success, even though others saw him as already being successful.

Some weeks later, he reported another dream:

While preparing to make a journey that would lead to my death, I was looking over some treasured items that I intended to bequeath to family members.

As he worked with this extremely powerful dream, he concluded that the part of himself that was preparing to "die" was the outgrown self who had accepted his parents' fears. By bequeathing to younger family members the "treasures" he had accumulated, he hoped to leave behind a more expansive and secure vision than the one he had inherited. After processing this second dream, he believed that he had successfully trans-

20

formed the old fears and reservations about success that had burdened his family for years, perhaps even for generations.

As this businessman discovered, actively engaging in dream transformation will increase your feeling of command over waking-life events. Instead of being the victim of circumstances, you become a creative participant—shaping inner and outer circumstances to fit your deepest wishes and desires.

Part Two
An Index of Basic Dream Images

Comments

All the items included in this index are organized alphabetically. But because it is often helpful to read over the associations for related items, there are several categories where, for easier reference, I have grouped together closely related images under subheadings. These categories include:

Animals, domestic
Animals, wild
Body parts
Clothing
Colors
Elements
House
Numbers
Sex
Vehicles
Water

All the items in these categories are also listed individually, in their proper alphabetical places.

For example, if your dream features the image of a dripping faucet, look up Water. You will find the subheading *dripping,* along with more information about the different meanings for water and emotion in dreams. These additional associations and questions will often help you relate that single dream to a much larger dream sequence.

Image:	Associations:	Ask Yourself:
Abandonment	Isolation. Leaving behind an old self. Release from control of the old self.	What part of me am I ready to leave behind?
Aborigine *See also* Native.	Intuitive self. Magical identity. Primordial wisdom.	Where in my life do I seek alignment with natural forces?
Abortion	Loss of the new. Failure to nurture.	What part of myself do I feel is too weak to survive?
Above	Higher self. Greater understanding or knowledge.	What do I aspire to? What do I want to know?
Abuse	Fear-induced violence.	What fears do I hide with anger?
Abyss	Vast depth. Profundity. Infinity.	What lies deep within me?
Accident	Unexpected change. Upset.	Where am I avoiding change?
Acorn *See* Seed.		
Acting *or* actor	Role. Desire for recognition.	What role am I playing? Do I feel unrecognized?

Addict *or* addiction	Obsessive need. Lack of control.	What habit is a threat to me?
Adolescent	Lusty stage of development. Rapid growth. Immaturity.	What part of me is almost there? Where in my life is my growth most intense?
Adopting *See also* Foundling; Orphan.	Work on creative production.	What is being born in me against all odds?
Adultery *See* Extramarital sex; Sex.		
Aerobics *See* Exercise.		
Affair *See also* Sex.	Surrender. Ardor.	What do I wish to yield to?
African-American	Freedom from repression.	In what way am I ready to be more expressive and creative?
Age *See* Old; Young.		

Image:	Associations:	Ask Yourself:
Agreement	If good agreement, harmony or commitment. If bad, compromise.	What do I wish to resolve? What am I willing to settle?
AIDS *See also* Plague.	Hopelessness. Self-denial or guilt. Dependency.	Am I ready to stop condemning myself and others?
Air *See also* Elements; Wind.	Breath. Intelligence. Force of mind.	What area of my life requires stimulation?
Airplane *See* Plane.		
Alcohol	Relaxation. Indulgence. Freedom from responsibility.	What do I want to release?
Alien *See also* UFO.	Distant, strange, or unrecognized. Nonhuman.	What part of me is strange or unconventional?
Alley	Life's passage. A narrow or secret way.	What choices am I ready to make public?
Alligator *See also* Animals, wild.	Primordial fear.	What elemental fears am I feeling?

Altar	Holiness. Sacrifice.	What do I worship? Do I want to give something up?
Ambulance	Rescue. Swift response.	What part of myself wants to save or be saved?
America *or* American	Vigor. Ingenuity. The New World. Innocence or naïveté. Patriotism.	What am I exploring? What new world lies within me?
Anal sex *See also* Sex.	Submission. Union without issue.	To what or to whom do I want or fear to yield?
Ancestor	Inherited traits.	What qualities do I wish to preserve or be free of?
Anchor	Security. Stability.	Where in my life do I wish to hold fast?
Angel	Transcendent knowledge. Compassion. Higher consciousness. Revelation.	What inspiration am I ready to receive?
Anger *See* Rage.		
Animals, domestic *See also subheadings.*	The natural self tamed by civilizing values.	What part of me is ready to be tamed? Or wishes it were not so domesticated?

Image:	Associations:	Ask Yourself:
—*bull*	Fertility and strength. Rage.	What incites my passion?
—*calf*	Immaturity. Callowness.	What qualities do I wish to develop?
—*camel*	Ship of the desert. Endurance.	What emotional resources am I conserving?
—*cat*	A feminine aspect. Cuddly and soft. Also independent and able to care for itself.	How am I integrating the yielding and independent parts of my nature? How do I feel about these qualities combined in a woman?
—*colt*	Potential. Gawkiness. Charm.	Where in my life am I beginning to realize my potential?
—*cow*	Docile and productive. Nurturing, if passive, aspect of self.	Am I passive? What do I nurture?
—*dog*	Usually a masculine aspect. Unconditional love. Obedient, loyal, trustworthy.	Am I trustworthy? What do I love unconditionally?
—*donkey*	Simplicity. Sturdiness.	Where in my life can I express my strength more directly?

30

—*goat*	Lusty vigor. Relentless energy. Omnivorous.	What am I determined to do?
—*goose*	Silly. Aggressive. Watchful.	Am I silly? Where in my life is my aggression apt to break out?
—*guinea pig*	Fecundity. Responsibleness.	What am I learning to care for?
—*hamster*	Dependency. Cuteness.	What part of me needs to be cared for?
—*horse* See also Vehicles.	Swift. Usually elegant. Feeling of developed consciousness. Sometimes unexpressed sexuality.	How do I feel about my power? What natural force am I suppressing or expressing?
—*horse, flying or winged*	Soaring consciousness. Limitless nature of self.	What part of me is ready to soar?
—*mule*	Obstinate. Intractable. Stamina.	Where in my life am I ready to persevere?
—*ox*	Burden. Strength. Stupidity.	How do I doubt my own strength? What makes me feel stupid?
—*pet*	Work on self-love.	What part of myself do I care for?
—*pig*	Greedy. Smart. Sometimes slovenly, sometimes fastidious.	Am I grabbing more than I need or can use? Did I clean up my own mess?

Image:	Associations:	Ask Yourself:
—*rabbit*	Fertility. Luck. Insecurity.	Where in my life am I ready to be productive?
—*sheep*	Conformity.	What am I following?
—*talking animal*	Magical communication. Natural wisdom.	What part of my nature has a message for me?
—*toy animal*	Playful relationship with the natural world. Freedom from responsibility.	Where do I want more pleasure in my life?
Animals, wild *See also subheadings.*	Natural, untamed self. Freedom from civilization.	What part of me seeks free expression?
—*alligator*	Primordial fear.	What elemental fears am I feeling?
—*ape*	Dexterity. Mischief. Humor.	What part of me is almost human?
—*armadillo*	Codependency.	What boundaries do I want or need to establish?
—*bat*	Nocturnal. Eerie. Keenly sensitive.	What darkness am I ready to navigate or explore?

32

—bear	Possessive love.	How am I threatened by love?
—coyote	Trickster. Rogue. Thief.	What adventures do I seek?
—crocodile See Animals, wild: alligator.		
—deer	Gentle beauty. Timidity.	What part of me hunts for protection?
—dinosaur	Fantasy. The power of size.	What part of me wants to be larger?
—dolphin	Natural intelligence. Transcendent wisdom. Compassion. Playfulness.	What part of me is divinely wise and playful?
—dragon	Mastery of elements. Abundance. Matter and spirit combined.	In what ways am I ready to align the physical and spiritual aspects of my nature?
—elephant	Wisdom. Memory. The power of persistence.	Where does my wisdom lie?
—fox	Cleverness. Cunning.	What do I trust, or not trust, in myself?
—frog	Transformation.	What beauty lies within me?

Image:	Associations:	Ask Yourself:
—*giraffe*	Overview. Shy grace.	Where in my life am I ready to extend my vision?
—*gorilla*	Strength. Innocence. Rarity.	In what areas of my life am I ready to be strong and gentle?
—*hippopotamus*	Vast strength. Hidden danger. Size.	How do I conceal my power?
—*lion*	Nobility. Strength. Pride.	Where does courage dwell in me?
—*lizard*	Cold-blooded. Reptilian.	Where in my life am I ready to show more warmth?
—*maggot* See Worm.		
—*monkey*	Dexterity. Mischief. Humor.	What part of me is almost human?
—*mouse*	Meek nature. Quiet. Minor problems. Inner feelings. Shyness.	What small troubles are gnawing away at me?
—*opossum*	Feigning death.	What threatens me? Where am I ready to come to life?
—*panther*	Wild beauty. Grace.	What force do I wish or fear to unleash?

—rabbit	Fertility. Luck. Insecurity.	Where in my life am I ready to be productive?
—rat	Street smarts. Clever. Sneaky and untrustworthy.	Where in my life do I fear betrayal? Can I trust myself?
—rhinoceros	Blind strength. Armoring.	What am I ready to see or understand about my power?
—seal	Comic instinct. Playfulness.	Where do I seek more joy in life?
—skunk	Passive aggression.	Where in my life do I feel the need to protect myself?
—snake	Energy. The serpent power of kundalini. Sexuality.	What energy am I ready to express or understand?
—squirrel	Hoarding. Running in place.	Where in my life am I ready to feel more secure?
—tiger	Power. Wild beauty. Sexual force.	What is dangerous in me?
—toad	Infectious ugliness.	How or why have I concealed my true beauty?
—toy wild animal	Playful relationship with what is wild. Trust.	In what areas of my life am I ready to trust?

Image:	Associations:	Ask Yourself:
—turtle	Protection. Perseverance.	Where in my life do I feel safe when I take my time?
—walrus	Massive sensitivity.	Where in my life am I ready to be less threatening?
—whale	Power of the unconscious. Truth and strength of inner being.	What great truth am I ready to accept?
—wolf	Instinct. Appetite. Threat. Loyalty.	What instincts are a threat to me? What are my instinctive loyalties?
—yeti	Man-beast. Legendary.	What part of my greater self is stalking me?
—zoo animal	Wildness under control.	What instincts do I want to observe or enjoy in safety?
Ankle *See also* Body parts.	Support. Direction.	Where am I going?
Ant	Social organization. Order. Industry.	How must I cooperate to achieve my desires?

Antique	Age. Survival value.	What part of me improves with age?
Anus *See also* Body parts.	Elimination.	What do I want to get rid of?
Apartment *See also* House.	A part of the total house of self.	What part of myself do I occupy?
Ape *See also* Animals, wild.	Dexterity. Mischief. Humor.	What part of me is almost human?
Applause	Recognition. Acclaim.	Where am I ready to acknowledge myself or to seek acknowledgment?
Aquarium	Microcosm of emotion.	What feelings am I ready to display or to view?
Arch	Fulfillment of aspirations. Higher goals.	What direction is opening before me?
Archaeology	Rediscovery of the past.	What ancient knowledge do I want to recover?
Architect	Work on design of new self or identity.	What plans am I making?

37

Image:	Associations:	Ask Yourself:
Arctic *See also* Ice; Frozen; North; Snow.	Purity. Isolation. Frozen feelings.	What is frozen or melting within me?
Arm *See also* Body parts.	Strength. To be prepared.	What am I ready for or getting ready for? What am I ready to give or receive?
Armadillo *See also* Animals, wild.	Armoring. Codependency.	What boundaries do I want or need to establish?
Arousal *See also* Sex.	Stimulation. Availability.	What do I want to respond to?
Arrest	Enforced stop. Being caught.	Why do I fear being caught? What do I want to stop?
Arrow	Hitting the mark. Cupid's dart. Painful realization.	What is the point?
Arson *See also* Fire.	Destructive rage. Cleansing anger.	What must I burn away in order to be free?
Art	Image of reality. Value. Creativity.	How do I express myself? What do I value?

Art gallery   Creative display.   What is uniquely mine? What am I ready for the world to view?

Artist   Work on creativity and originality.   What part of me is ready for expression? Where am I unique?

Ashes   Remains.   What is over for me? What am I ready to discard?

Asia *or* Asian   Wisdom. Subtlety. Inscrutability.   Where does my wisdom lie? What do I keep to myself?

Ass
See Animals, domestic: *donkey, mule;* Buttocks.

Asthma   Loss of emotional security.   What part of myself am I preparing to care for?

Astrology
See Zodiac.

Athlete   Work on physical energy. Strength. Skill. Honor.   What abilities do I want to develop or be recognized for?

39

Image:	Associations:	Ask Yourself:
Atom bomb	Destruction on a vast scale.	What am I ready to end? What do I fear is ending?
Attic *See also* House.	Higher consciousness. Memory. Stored-up past.	What is "up there" that I want—or fear—to explore?
Attorney	Advocacy. Resolution of conflict.	Where in my life do I need help? What issues am I ready to resolve?
Autumn *See* Fall.		
Avalanche	Catastrophic release of unexpressed emotion.	What old emotions are about to break away forcefully?
Axe	Powerful severing.	What am I ready to chop away?
Baby *See also* Blue baby.	Infant self. Rebirth. Trust.	What is being born or reborn in me? What do I trust?
Baby-sitter	Work on inner child.	How am I preparing to care for the child inside of me?
Back *See also* Body parts.	Unconscious. "Back there."	What is going on that I can't see?

Backpack	Easy-to-carry opinions or responsibilities. Survival.	What can I conveniently carry? How well do my beliefs fit together?
Backpacking *See also* Camping.	Work on self-sufficiency.	What can I do without? What must I carry with me to survive?
Baggage *See also* Luggage.	Opinions. Attitudes. Material goods and responsibilities.	What am I carrying with me? How do I feel about the load?
Bag lady *See also* Bum.	Insecurity. Failure. Loss of identity.	In what way is my identity or success threatened?
Balcony	Viewing. Seeing or being seen.	What do I wish to safely observe? How do I choose to be seen?
Bald *See also* Hair.	Sexual issues. Wisdom.	What do I want to give up, or fear to lose?
Ball	Integration. Wholeness.	What parts of my being am I uniting?
Ballet *See also* Dancing.	Disciplined grace. Culture.	Where in my life is my strength taking form? How do I wish to express it?

Image:	Associations:	Ask Yourself:
Ball game *See also* Sports.	Integration of individual and collective consciousness. Wholesome competition.	What do I want to be a part of? What group am I aligning myself with?
Balloon	Lightheartedness. Joyfulness.	What makes my spirits rise?
Bamboo	Versatility. Exuberant growth. Strength. Flexibility.	Where in my life am I ready to flourish? What boundaries have I overstepped?
Bandage	Protection. Desire for healing.	What part of me am I ready to heal or take care of?
Band-Aid *See* Bandage.		
Bank	Preservation of resources.	What do I want to save or to keep secure?
Banquet	Formal celebration. Recognition.	What acknowledgment do I need to feel nourished?
Bar *See also* Tavern.	Relaxation. Indulgence. Irresponsibility. Pleasure.	Where in my life do I feel overloaded or stressed out?

Bark
See also Skin; Tree.

Outer covering. Protection.

How can I find the balance between oversensitivity and insensitivity?

Barn

Storage. Home to animal nature.

What part of me needs to feel cared for or safe?

Barrel

Containment. Capacity.

What am I storing? How much can I hold?

Baseball
See Ball game; Sports.

Basement
See also House.

Below. The unconscious.

What part of my unconscious is ready to be seen?

Basket

Pliability. Craftsmanship.

Where in my life must I be flexible in order to carry on?

Basketball
See Ball game; Sports.

Bat
See also Animals, wild.

Nocturnal. Eerie. Keenly sensitive.

What darkness am I ready to navigate?

Bath *or* bathing

Cleansing. Release.

What do I want to wash away?

Image:	Associations:	Ask Yourself:
Bathing suit *See also* Bikini; Clothing; Swim- ming; Water.	Uncovered. Confidence.	What feelings am I ready to disclose?
Bathroom *See also* House.	Place of cleansing and release.	What am I ready to let go of?
Battle *See also* War.	Conflict. Struggle.	What parts of me are at war?
Bay *See also* Harbor; Water.	Shelter. Enclosure.	Where do I feel calm?
Beach	Where conscious and unconscious meet.	What am I ready to be conscious of?
Bear *See also* Animals, wild.	Possessive love.	How am I threatened by love?
Beard	Authority. Power. Wisdom.	How do I express power? How is my authority shown?

44

Beatnik	Rejection of social values. Isolation.	In what ways am I willing to stand alone?
Bed	Sleep. Rest. Retreat from activity. Foundation.	What do I wish to retreat or rest from?
Bedroom *See also* House.	Privacy. Rest. Intimacy.	What is my inner reality?
Bee	Activity. Productivity. Social life.	Where in my life do I get a buzz?
Beef *See* Meat.		
Beer *See also* Alcohol; Drunk.	Conviviality. Refreshment.	What do I need to relax?
Beige *See also* Colors.	Neutrality. Detachment. Absence of communication. Status.	What am I ready to take more seriously, or be less serious about?
Bell	Signal. Recognition. Celebration.	What do I want to hear or fear to hear?
Belt *See also* Clothing.	Holding up. Securing. Linking.	What am I ready to connect?

45

Image:	Associations:	Ask Yourself:
Bestiality *See also* Sex.	Union with animal passions or instinct.	What basic aspects of myself do I fear or deny?
Bicycle *See also* Vehicles.	Self-propulsion. Recreation.	Do I have enough strength to make it? Will it be fun?
Big	Larger than usual. Inflated. Generous.	Where in my life am I ready to expand? Where do I fear overexpansion?
Bigfoot *See* Yeti.		
Bikini *See also* Bathing suit; Clothing.	Exposure. Display. Revealing.	What am I ready to lay bare?
Bill	Payment due.	What has to be paid for?
Billfold *See also* Clothing.	Masculine security. Resources. Identity.	What feelings about security am I ready to change?
Bird	Freedom. Escape. Liberation from weight of physical plane.	What part of me wants to fly?
Birth *See* Baby.		

Birthday	Celebration of beginnings.	What is born in me?
Black *See also* Colors.	Isolation. Boundary. Separation. Introspection. Transition color.	What am I separating myself from?
Black person *See also* African-American.		
Blanket	Comfort. Security. Warmth.	What discomfort or fear am I covering up?
Blind	Unseeing. Unaware.	What am I ready to see or to comprehend?
Blond *See also* Brunette; Redhead.	Glamour. Artifice. Frivolity.	What part of me wants to enjoy life more?
Blood	Essence. Life energy. Threat to life.	Where in my life is my vitality spilling out?
Blossom *See* Flower.		
Blouse *See also* Clothing.	Upper, as opposed to lower, self. Emotions.	What feelings do I consider appropriate?

47

Image:	Associations:	Ask Yourself:
Blue *See also* Colors.	Harmony. Spirituality. Inner peace. Devotion.	What is the source of my peace?
Blue baby *See also* Baby.	Weakness of trust. Threat to innocence.	What is feeble about my beliefs or faith?
Blue jeans *See also* Clothing.	Community. Comfort. Freedom.	Where in my life am I at ease? Where do I want to be more at ease?
Boat *See also* Vehicle.	Movement across the depths of feeling.	What emotions can I safely navigate?
Body parts *See also subheadings.*	External form of internal nature.	What part is important?
—*ankle*	Support. Direction.	Where am I going?
—*anus*	Elimination.	What do I want to get rid of?
—*arm*	Strength. To be prepared.	What am I ready for or getting ready for? What am I ready to give or receive?
—*back*	Unconscious. "Back there."	What is going on that I can't see?

—*brain*	Intellect. Mind. Reason.	What am I ready to understand?
—*breast*	Nurturing. Female sexuality. Maternal love.	What am I nurturing? What part of me needs to be loved?
—*buttocks*	Humility. Stupidity. Power.	Am I being an ass? What do I need to forgive in myself?
—*chest* *See also* Body parts: *heart, lungs.*	Fullness of life. Generosity.	What do I want to experience fully?
—*ear*	Receptivity.	What am I open to? What am I ready to hear?
—*eye*	Vision. Consciousness. Clarity.	What am I aware of? How do I see the world?
—*eyelashes*	Protection of vision. Allure.	How well do I see? What can I safely observe? What do I show to the world?
—*face*	Identity. Ego. Self-image.	How do I appear?
—*finger*	Sensitivity. Awareness.	What am I touching?

49

Image:	Associations:	Ask Yourself:
—*fingernails*	Safe handling. Glamorous or functional.	What am I prepared to handle, or what do I wish to avoid doing?
—*foot*	Grounding. Direction. Basic beliefs.	Where am I going?
—*guts*	Fortitude. Stamina.	From what source do I draw my strength?
—*hair*	Protection. Attraction. Sensuality.	What am I covering? What do I display?
—*hand*	Capacity. Competence. Help.	What am I ready to handle?
—*head*	Intellect. Understanding. Superior.	What am I ready to understand?
—*heart*	Love. Security.	Where in my life am I ready to give and receive love?
—*jaw*	Will. Relentless anger.	Where in my life must I dominate? Where am I ready to yield?
—*knee*	Flexibility. Humility.	Where in my life do I need to bend?

—*leg* — Support. Movement. — What supports me? Am I getting somewhere?

—*lungs* — Breath of life. Freedom. — In what ways is my life ready to expand?

—*mouth* — Nourishment. New attitudes. — What am I ready to take in? What am I ready to express?

—*muscles* — Power. Strength. — In what aspects of my life am I ready to be more powerful?

—*neck* — Flexibility, especially of vision. — What can I see if I make a small adjustment?

—*nose* — Instinctive knowledge. — How does it smell to me? What do I know without knowing?

—*penis* — Male sexuality. Yang power. — How is my power expressed?

—*scalp*
See Body parts: *skin, hair.*

—*shoulders* — Strength or burdens. — What am I ready to carry? What is too heavy for me?

52

Image:	Associations:	Ask Yourself:
—*skeleton*	Work on support or structure. Remains.	Where in my life do I feel disconnected or falling apart?
—*skin*	Surface of the self. Sensitivity. Connection between inner and outer.	What is on the surface?
—*spine*	Support. Responsibility.	What holds me up?
—*stomach*	Digestion of information or circumstances. Understanding.	What value can I receive from my experience?
—*teeth*	Independence. Power. Ability to nourish and communicate.	Where in my life do I fear dependence? What do I wish to say?
—*testicles*	Yang power. Masculinity.	What power am I ready to express?
—*thigh*	Power of movement.	Am I strong enough to get where I want to go?
—*throat*	Communication. Creativity. Trust.	What am I ready to hear and say?
—*toe*	Beginning, especially of movement.	Where am I preparing to go?

—tongue	The pleasure of taste.	What am I eager to try?
—vagina	Female sexuality. Yin receptivity.	What do I receive? What receives me?
Bomb	Explosive energy.	What is ready to explode?
Bondage	Restriction. Forceful limitation.	What am I afraid I might do?
Bone	Structure. Evidence. Support.	What supports me? Where do I look for support?
Bonnet *See also* Clothing.	Sheltered or old-fashioned beliefs.	Where or how is my vision restricted?
Book	Information. Guidance. Record keeping.	What am I trying to find out? Where am I looking?
Bookstore	Current information. Available knowledge.	What information am I shopping around for?
Boots *See also* Clothing.	Power of movement. Vigor.	What form of power do I seek?
Border	Where two states, attitudes, or life patterns meet.	What new area am I preparing to cross into?
Boss	Power. Direction. Control.	Where in my life am I ready or reluctant to take charge?

53

Image:	Associations:	Ask Yourself:
Bottom *See also* Under.	Foundation. Completion.	What have I explored fully? What do I wish to explore fully?
Boulder	Barrier. Building block.	What blocks my way? How can I use the material that has blocked my path?
Box	Enclose. Contain. Store.	What do I want to keep safe?
Boxer	Work on power or confrontation.	What rules must I follow to be comfortable expressing my power?
Boxing	Strength. Power. Stamina.	Where in my life do I wish to be strong or assertive?
Boy	Yang power developing.	Where is power growing for me?
Boyfriend	Masculine ideal.	What do I admire in a man? What qualities am I ready to integrate?
Bra *See also* Breasts; Clothing.	Private feminine self.	How do I express my femininity?

Bracelet *See also* Jewelry.	Binding. Commitment.	What do I wish to display?
Brakes *See also* Vehicles.	Control or slowing of movement.	Where in my life am I ready to feel more secure with my power?
Brain *See also* Body parts.	Intellect. Mind. Reason.	What am I ready to understand?
Branches	Extension of growth.	In what direction am I growing?
Brassiere *See* Bra.		
Bread *See also* Food.	Sustenance. Shared resources. Uniting.	What fellowship nourishes me?
Breaking	Destruction. Forceful change.	What patterns or forms have I outgrown?
Breast *See also* Body parts.	Nurturing. Female sexuality. Maternal love.	What am I nurturing? What part of me needs to be loved?
Bricks	Solidity.	What am I building to last?
Bride	Feminine receptivity.	What am I ready to receive?
Bridge	Connection. Overcoming problems.	What am I ready to cross?

Image:	Associations:	Ask Yourself:
Briefcase	Attitudes and beliefs about work and business. Professional identity.	How does my work fulfill or limit me?
Brother	Masculine aspect of self. Fellowship.	What do I admire or fear in myself?
Brown *See also* Colors.	Material world. Security.	What needs organization in my life?
Brunette *See also* Blond; Redhead.	Sultry. Natural. Practical.	Where in my life do I want to be down-to-earth?
Bubble	Soaring. Release. Unreal expectations.	Where in my life am I ready to rise? Do I fear my expectations will not be fulfilled?
Bucket	Container.	What feelings can I easily handle?
Bud	Putting forth.	What is emerging from within me?
Bug	Minor problems. Inconvenience.	What bugs me?

Bull *See also* Animals, domestic.	Fertility and strength. Rage.	What incites my passion?
Bulldozer	Elemental changes.	What basic changes am I preparing to make?
Bum *See also* Bag lady.	Failure. Outcast. Loss of control.	Where do I feel I am losing control of my life?
Burial *See also* Death; Funeral.	Return to earth.	What am I ready to lay to rest?
Burning	Consuming energy. Fiery release.	Where am I most passionate?
Bus *See also* Vehicles.	Shared journey. Mass transit.	How does my personal power relate to mass consciousness?
Butter	Richness. Flavor.	What gratification am I hungry for?
Butterfly	Beauty. Freedom. Transformation.	What am I ready to change into?
Buttocks *See also* Body parts.	Humility. Stupidity. Power.	Am I being an ass? What do I need to forgive in myself?

Image:	Associations:	Ask Yourself:
Buzzard *See* Vulture.		
Cabin *See* Cottage.		
Cage	Imprisoning of dangerous elements.	What part of me must I control or limit? In what ways am I dangerous?
Cake	Celebration. Sometimes treat, sometimes indulgence.	Do I deserve a treat? Can I indulge myself?
Calf *See also* Animals, domestic.	Immaturity. Callowness.	What qualities do I wish to develop?
Calm	Tranquillity. Stillness.	What makes me feel centered?
Camel *See also* Animals, domestic.	Ship of the desert. Endurance.	What emotional resources am I conserving?
Camera	Image of experience. Record. Sometimes a means of distancing.	How does it look to me? Do I want to be involved?

Term	Meaning	Question
Camp fire *See also* Fire.	Companionship. Shared energy.	What companions do I seek?
Camping *See also* Backpacking.	Natural living. Back to basics.	Have I denied basic needs? Am I well grounded?
Can	Preservation.	What do I want to keep?
Cancer	Destructive growth.	What part of me is out of control?
Candle	Illumination. Search for vision.	What do I want to see?
Candy *See also* Sugar.	Small treats. Temptation.	Do I receive what is essential to me?
Cane *See also* Cripple; Crutches; Disabled.	Limitation. Restriction.	What inhibits my free movement?
Cannibal	Part of the self sacrificed to the rest. Fear of integration.	What part of me is consuming?
Canyon	A channel in the flow of consciousness. Passageway.	What feelings flow through me?
Cap *See also* Clothing.	Informal. Liberal opinions.	Where in my life do I want to be more tolerant?

Image:	Associations:	Ask Yourself:
Cape *See also* Clothing.	Dramatic protection. Fantasy.	What part am I playing?
Car *See also* Vehicles.	Personal power. Ego.	Can I get there? Who am I?
Cards	Skill and chance.	What game am I playing?
Carnival	Uninhibited fun. Freedom from restraint.	Where in my life do I want to cut loose?
Carousel *See also* Merry-go-round.		
Carpet	Protection. Insulation. Sometimes luxury or richness.	Where in my life am I ready to expand beyond my basic needs?
Car phone *See also* Cellular phone; Car; Telephone.		
Cartoon character	Caricature.	What elements of myself do I find amusing or foolish?
Castle *See also* House.	Fortified but noble self.	What walls am I ready to remove?

60

Castration *See also* Eunuch.	Denial of sexuality. Limitation of creative power.	What is threatening about my creativity or my sexuality?
Cat *See also* Animals, domestic.	A feminine aspect. Cuddly and soft. Also independent and able to care for itself.	How am I integrating the yielding and independent parts of my nature? How do I feel about these qualities combined in a woman?
Catalogue	Opportunity. Options. Convenience.	What can I easily obtain?
Cave	Inner or hidden issues. Female sexuality. The past.	What is inside that I wish to explore?
Caveman *or* **cavewoman**	Primordial aspect of self.	What is fundamental to my nature?
Ceiling *See also* House.	Upper limits.	Where in my life am I ready to raise my limits?
Celebrity	Recognition. Fame. Sometimes notoriety.	What part of me wants to be recognized? Do I fear recognition?
Cellar *See* Basement.		

Image:	Associations:	Ask Yourself:
Cellular phone	Accessible, expansive communication.	What communication is of vital importance to me?
Cemetery	Death. Transformation.	What is over for me?
Centaur *See also* Horse; Man.	Union of animal and human nature, or of instincts and consciousness.	Where in my life am I integrating natural wisdom with intellect? What aspect of my sexual nature am I healing?
Center	Focus point. Quintessence.	What is my inmost nature?
Centipede	Poisonous feelings, thoughts, words.	What fears are restricting my progress?
Ceremony	Formal rite. Ritual.	What deep commitment am I ready to make?
Cesspool *See also* Sewer.	Accumulated negativity. Recycling.	What am I filtering out?
Chain	Bonds. The strength of many.	What restricts or strengthens me?
Chainsaw	Forceful severing.	What must I rip apart or cut down?

Chair	Position, style, or attitude.	What am I comfortable with?
Chalice	Inner wholeness. Spiritual self.	What spiritual thirst am I ready to quench?
Chandelier	Splendor of illumination.	What is my grand vision?
Channeling	Mediumship. Communication with higher realms.	What part of my greater self is ready to speak?
Charge card *See* Credit card.		
Chasing	Pursuit.	Where in my life do I deny my own power? What am I ready to catch?
Chasm *See* Abyss.		
Check *See also* Checkbook.	Convenient resources. Safety.	How do I protect my resources?
Checkbook *See also* Check.	Available resources. Convenient money.	What are my available means?
Cherub	Divine innocence. Angelic child.	Where is my spirit reborn?

63

Image:	Associations:	Ask Yourself:
Chest *See also* Body parts: *heart, lungs.*	Fullness of life. Generosity.	What do I want to experience fully?
Chicken *See also* Animals, domestic.	Scattered, disorganized thoughts. Small fears.	Where do I need to focus my awareness? Am I needlessly fearful?
Child *or* children	Innocence. The new self seeking to develop.	Where in my life am I developing? What part of my nature is childlike?
China *See* Dishes.		
Chiropractor	Work on structure or support.	What part of me wants to be strong?
Chocolate	Gratification. Indulgence. Pleasure.	What do I want or fear to indulge in?
Choking	Restricted communication.	What am I afraid to say?
Christ *See also* Jesus.	Higher consciousness. Salvation.	What part of me is divine? How do I experience my own divinity?

Christmas	Celebration. Holiday spirit of festivity and light. Reunion.	What am I celebrating? What do I wish to reunite with?
Church	Spiritual belief. Organized religion.	What is the structure of my belief?
Cigarette *See also* Smoking.	Stimulation. Addiction.	What do I seek distraction from?
Circle	Whole. Repetition. Infinity.	What is complete?
Circus	Childlike joy. Fantasy. Profusion.	What do I want to enjoy?
City	Civilized order. Culture. Community or decay of systems.	How do my parts cooperate or fail to cooperate?
Classroom *See also* School.	Work on education or training.	What am I ready to learn?
Claw *See also* Animals, domestic; Animals, wild.	Threatening animal instincts.	What fears am I preparing to confront?
Clay	Receptive matter.	What am I ready to form or mold?

Image:	Associations:	Ask Yourself:
Cleaning	Restoration of order. Purification. Maintenance.	What do I care for or what am I restoring?
Cliff	Challenge. Precipitous height.	What do I aspire to?
Climbing	Aspiration. Growth with effort. Achievement.	What am I trying to reach?
Clinic	Detached attitude toward health and well-being.	What attachments are blocking my good health?
Cloak *See also* Clothing.	Magical protection. Secrecy.	What part of me is invisible?
Clock *See also* Time; Watch.	Timing. Measurement.	How much time do I have? What is running out?
Closet	Storage of ideas or identity.	What is put away?
Clothing *See also* subheadings.	Identity. Self-image. Exploration of new roles or rejection of old.	What part of myself do I choose to show?
—*bathing suit*	Uncovered. Confident.	What feelings am I ready to disclose?
—*belt*	Holding up. Securing. Linking.	What am I ready to connect?
—*bikini*	Exposure. Display. Revealing.	What am I ready to lay bare?

—billfold	Masculine security. Resources. Identity.	What feelings about security am I ready to change?
—blouse	Upper, as opposed to lower, self. Emotions.	What feelings do I consider appropriate?
—blue jeans	Community. Comfort. Freedom.	Where in my life am I at ease? Where do I want to be more at ease?
—bonnet	Sheltered or old-fashioned beliefs.	Where or how is my vision restricted?
—boots	Power of movement. Vigor.	What form of power do I seek?
—bra	Private feminine self.	How do I express my femininity?
—cap	Informal. Liberal opinions.	Where in my life do I want to be more tolerant?
—cape	Dramatic protection. Fantasy.	What part am I playing?
—cloak	Magical protection. Secrecy.	What part of me is invisible?
—coat	Protection. Covering.	What am I covering up?
—dress	Self-image. Feminine self.	Who am I? How feminine am I?

67

Image:	Associations:	Ask Yourself:
—*handbag* See Clothing: *purse.*		
—*hat*	Opinions. Thoughts.	What thoughts or attitudes do I reveal?
—*helmet* See also Clothing: *hat.*	Protected opinions and attitudes.	What thoughts or opinions am I ready to change?
—*high heels*	Glamour. Restriction. Sexual invitation.	How comfortable am I with conventional femininity?
—*jacket*	Freedom of movement. Adventure.	Where in my life do I seek liberty of action?
—*laundry*	Cleansing. Purification. Release.	What am I ready to clean up? What has been sullied through use?
—*nightgown* See Clothing: *dress*; Night.		
—*overalls*	Common. Sturdiness. Protection.	What do I cover? What work is hard for me?

—*panties* *See also* Clothing: *underwear.*	Private self. Sexual identity.	What are my hidden feelings? What am I ready to expose?
—*playsuit*	Child aspect of self.	Where in my life do I want more enjoyment?
—*purse*	Feminine self. Sometimes sexual identity. Security.	What am I holding onto? What part of myself do I value?
—*shirt*	Upper, as opposed to lower, self. Emotions.	What feelings do I consider appropriate?
—*shoes*	General situation. Grounding.	How well do I connect with the world?
—*shorts* *See* Clothing: *underwear.*		
—*skirt* or *trousers*	Lower self. Passions.	What signals am I sending?
—*slip*	Private or inner self.	What do I wish or fear to reveal to the world?
—*suit*	Formality. Professional identity.	What power or ability do I wish to be recognized for?

Image:	Associations:	Ask Yourself:
—*sundress*	Comfortable exposure.	What pleasures am I seeking? What part of me is ready to relax?
—*tights*	Shaping. Firming.	What can I safely expose?
—*trousers* see Clothing: skirt or trousers.		
—*underwear*	Private self. Sexual identity.	What are my hidden feelings? What am I ready to expose?
—*uniform*	Conformity.	Where in my life do I wish to share with others? Where do I want to break free of rules?
—*veil*	Illusion. Mystery.	What do I want to hide or to reveal?
Clouds	Transition. May be dark or light. Confusion.	What am I moving through?
Clown	Healing through laughter. Often bittersweet joy.	Must I suffer to be happy?
Club	Joining together. Fellowship.	What do I wish to belong to?

Coal	Unrefined matter. Source of heat. Potential diamonds.	What potential lies within me?
Coat	Protection. Covering.	What am I covering up?
See also Clothing.		
Cobra		
See Snake.		
Cobweb		
See Web.		
Cocaine		
See Drugs.		
Cocoon	Sheltered development. Safety.	What part of me needs protection in order to grow?
Coffee	Stimulation. Sometimes over-excitement. Communication.	What activates me? Where in my life do I need to slow down?
Coffin	Containing the end.	What am I ready to bury?
Coins	Small value. Lesser worth.	What is of significant value to me? Where in my life am I distracted by lesser concerns?

Image:	Associations:	Ask Yourself:
Cold	Emotional chill. Lack of circulation.	What warmth am I missing?
College *See* University.		
Colors *See subheadings.*		
—*beige*	Neutrality. Detachment. Absence of communication. Status.	What am I ready to take more seriously, or be less serious about?
—*black*	Isolation. Boundary. Separation. Introspection. Transition color.	What am I separating myself from?
—*blue*	Harmony. Spirituality. Inner peace. Devotion.	What is the source of my inner peace?
—*brown*	Material world. Security.	What needs organization in my life?
—*gray*	Transition from one state to another. If clear, peace. If dull, fear.	What am I moving toward?
—*green*	Growth. Serenity. Healing through growth.	Where in my life am I growing?

—orange	Emotion. Stimulation. Healing.	What am I feeling?
—pink	Affection. Love.	To what am I responding?
—purple See Colors: *violet*.		
—red	Energy. Vigor. Passion.	What is my source of energy or strength?
—tan	Convention. Hard work. Propriety.	In what ways do I seek or avoid respectability?
—turquoise	Healing. Good luck. Protection.	Where in my life do I feel safe?
—violet	Spirituality. Boundary between visible and invisible realms. Aristocracy.	To what do I aspire?
—white	Purity. Clarity. Coldness.	What do I seek to purify?
—yellow	Vitality. Intellect. Clarity.	What do I wish to understand?
Colt See *also* Animals, domestic.	Potential. Gawkiness. Charm.	Where in my life am I beginning to realize my potential?
Comet	Messenger. Awakening or unleashing of energy.	What vision do I seek?

Image:	Associations:	Ask Yourself:
Commune	Collective energy. Socialization. Union of beliefs.	What do I wish to join? Who are my peers?
Companion *See* Friend.		
Compost	Fertile refuse.	What richness is buried in my past?
Computer	Facility of communication. High technology.	What area of communication is opening up for me?
Concentration camp	Fear and hatred of differences.	What is unique in me? What do I share with all others?
Concert	Work on harmony. Cooperation.	In what way do I want to join with others?
Condom	Sexual protection. Silliness.	Do I feel safe or silly about sex?
Constipation	Fear of letting go.	What am I holding back?
Construction	Work on structure of self.	Where in my life am I ready to build anew?

Contest	Competition. Rivalry.	What strengths am I ready to display?
Convent	Spiritual community. Withdrawal from familial and worldly affairs.	What inner needs am I ready to nurture and support?
Convertible *See also* Vehicles.	Glamourous power. Parade.	What power am I ready to display?
Convulsions *See* Seizures.		
Cooking	Preparing to nourish.	What do I nourish in myself or others?
Cop *See* Police.		
Copier	Repetition. Ease of reproduction.	What message do I want to circulate?
Corner	No escape. Hidden. Unavoidable.	Where are my choices leading me?
Corridor *See* Hall.		

75

Image:	Associations:	Ask Yourself:
Corsage	Ornament of honor. Recognition.	What part of myself deserves or seeks to be acknowledged?
Costume *See* Disguise.		
Cottage *See also* House.	Cozy, familiar house of the self.	What part of me wants to be snug?
Counselor *See* Attorney *or* Therapist.		
Countries *See also* Foreign.	Alternative realities or attitudes.	Which of the qualities of this place do I find or seek in myself?
Country	Natural world. Space. Basic needs and desires.	Am I overcivilized? Do I feel confined by expectations?
Court	Resolution of problems. Conflict.	What issue am I ready to resolve? Where do I fear judgment?

Cow *See also* Animals, domestic.	Docile and productive. Nurturing, if passive, aspect of self.	Am I passive? What do I nurture?
Cowboy *or* cowgirl	Adventure. Romance. Independence.	What part of me wants to roam free?
Co-worker	Collaboration. Work on relationships.	How am I ready to be more cooperative? What is or isn't working for me?
Coyote *See also* Animals, wild.	Trickster. Rogue. Thief.	What adventure do I seek?
Crab	Soft meat, hard shell.	Am I too sensitive?
Crack *See also* Drugs.	Possibility.	What opportunity am I ready to seize?
Crash *See* Wreck.		
Crawling	Regressive movement.	In what areas of my life do I want to take my time?

77

Image:	Associations:	Ask Yourself:
Crazy	Total loss of control. Freedom from responsibility.	What holds me together? What happens if I lose it?
Credit card	Buy now, pay later. Ready access to resources. Protection.	What am I worth?
Creek *See also* Water.	The flow of feeling.	What feelings flow comfortably within me?
Crime	Guilt. Shame. Powerlessness.	What inner fear threatens me?
Criminal	Work on powerlessness.	Where in my life am I preparing to express my strength?
Cripple *See also* Disabled.	Disabled. Limitation.	What am I ready to heal?
Crocodile *See also* Alligator.		
Cross	Sacrifice. Suffering. Salvation.	What do I wish to transform?
Crossroad	Choice of direction.	Which way do I want to go?
Crowd	Throng of alternatives. Options.	What are my choices?

Crown	Majesty. To be chosen.	What part of me seeks acknowledgment?
Crutches *See also* Cripple; Disabled.	Insupportable weakness.	In what area am I seeking freedom of movement?
Crying	Emotional release. Grief.	What emotions am I ready to express?
Crystal	Essential self. Clarity. Focus.	What is essential to me?
Cult	Unquestioning devotion. Sometimes obsessive beliefs.	Which of my beliefs are ready to expand? Which of my beliefs are limiting me?
Cup	Receptiveness.	What am I ready to receive?
Cupboard	Storage. Hidden.	What do I want to keep safe? What am I ready to disclose?
Curtain	Protection. Decoration.	In what ways do I seek privacy? Or what do I wish to display?
Cut *See* Wound.		

79

Image:	Associations:	Ask Yourself:
Damage	Injury. Loss.	What am I ready to restore or replace?
Dancing *See also* Ballet.	Joyous participation in life. Movement as transcendence.	What inspires me to go beyond my imagined limits?
Danger	Threatening change.	What am I afraid to lose if I change?
Dark	Mystery. The unknown and unformed. A place of fear or of potential.	For what do I search? What seeks to take form?
Dart	Point of awareness.	What hits the target?
Daughter	Youthful feminine self.	In what area of my life am I ready to express youthful receptivity?
Dawn	Beginning. Understanding.	What is beginning?
Deaf	Work on communication.	What do I wish or fear to hear?
Death	End of a cycle.	What is over?
Debris	Fragments. Rubbish.	What do I wish to restore to wholeness?

Deck
Outdoor living. Connection between self and nature.

Where in my self do I seek alignment with nature?

Deer
See also Animals, wild.
Gentle beauty. Timidity.

What part of me hunts for protection?

Defecation
See also Bathroom.
Elimination. Dumping, especially of garbage from the past.

What am I ready to get rid of?

Deformity
Failure of expectation. Disappointment.

What part of myself am I ready to accept and love? Where in my life do I seek perfection?

Demolition
Work on elimination.

What part of my life is no longer functional?

Demon
See also Devil; Monster.
Image of self-doubt or denial.

What stands between me and greater consciousness?

Dentist
See also Teeth.
Work on independence and power.

What part of me needs strengthening?

Department store
See Store.

Image:	Associations:	Ask Yourself:
Depression	Suppressed emotion. Lack of options.	What am I afraid to feel?
Desert	Isolation. Retreat. Endurance.	What do I wish to withdraw from?
Designer	Organization. Form.	What new plans am I ready to formulate?
Desk	Organization. Getting down to business.	What am I ready to accomplish?
Dessert	Indulgence. Treats.	What gives me pleasure? Where are my needs unfulfilled?
Detached *See also* Unfeeling.		
Detour	Change of direction in life's path.	What must I avoid to reach my true destination?
Devil *See also* Demon.	Negative forces. Temptation.	What lies between me and my own greater consciousness?
Dew *See also* Water.	Gentle release of emotion.	What feelings can I safely express?

Diamond *See also* Jewel.	Purity. Clarity. Enduring treasure.	What is precious to me?
Diarrhea	Letting go.	What must I release?
Dictator	Control. Oppression.	In what ways can I be more flexible in making decisions?
Diet	Self-discipline or punishment. Self-restraint.	What must I give up or control to be healthy?
Dining room *See also* Food; House.	The ritual of eating. Formality.	What sustenance do I require?
Dinosaur *See also* Animals, wild.	Fantasy. The power of size.	What part of me wants to be larger?
Dirt *See also* Earth.	If negative, unclean; if positive, fertility.	What do I need to clean up? What part of me wants to grow?
Disabled *See also* Cripple.	Restriction. Disadvantage.	What part of me is ready to be made whole?
Disc	Preserving knowledge. Receptacle.	What information do I want to keep safe?

83

Image:	Associations:	Ask Yourself:
Disco *See* Dancing; Nightclub.		
Disguise	Hidden parts of self.	What am I concealing? What am I ready to reveal?
Dishes	Vessels of nourishment.	With what am I preparing to sustain myself?
Dismemberment	Pulling to pieces.	What must I pull apart in order to be together?
Ditch	Drainage. Escape.	What am I ready to clear away or escape from?
Diving	Plunging into emotional depths.	What feelings am I ready to fathom?
Dock	Safe landing.	What feelings have I safely navigated?
Doctor	Work on healing.	What part of me is ready to be healed?
Dog *See also* Animals, domestic.	Usually a masculine aspect. Unconditional love. Obedient, loyal, trustworthy.	Am I trustworthy? What do I love unconditionally?

Doll	Relationship practice.	In what areas of my life am I ready to be more caring?
Dolphin *See also* Animals, wild.	Natural intelligence. Transcendent wisdom. Compassion. Playfulness.	What part of me is divinely wise and playful?
Donkey *See also* Animals, domestic.	Simplicity. Sturdiness.	Where in my life can I express my strength more directly?
Door *See also* House.	Access. Movement from one area to another.	What space am I ready to enter or to keep private?
Dove	Peace. Resolution of conflict.	What problem am I ready to solve?
Down	Unconscious. Beneath.	What do I want to be aware of? What underlies my beliefs?
Dragon *See also* Animals, wild.	Mastery of elements. Abundance. Matter and spirit combined.	In what ways am I ready to align the physical and spiritual aspects of my nature?
Dragonfly	Freedom and beauty of spirit.	Where in my life am I ready to fly free?

Image:	Associations:	Ask Yourself:
Drapes *See* Curtain.		
Dreaming	Creating. Waking to inner reality.	What is real for me?
Dress *See also* Clothing.	Self-image. Feminine self.	Who am I? How feminine am I?
Dresser *See also* Cupboard.	Storage.	What do I want to keep safe?
Dripping *See also* Water.	Trickle of emotion.	What am I releasing, bit by bit?
Driveway	Access to power and movement.	How easily can I access my power?
Driving *See also* Traveling; Vehicles.	Work on energy and power.	How far can I go? What is my desired destination?
Drooling	Loss of control. Foolishness.	What do I take too seriously?

Drowning	Going under emotionally.	In what areas of my life am I ready to feel more emotionally secure?
Drugs	Healing or making insensible.	What do I want to stifle or to intensify?
Drunk	Total insensibility.	Where in my life do I fear—or wish—to lose control?
Dummy	Representation. Emptiness.	What is missing in my relationships? What am I lonely for?
Dump *See also* Garbage; Junkyard.	Refuse of living. Elimination.	What do I no longer need?
Dune	Timelessness. Mutability. Flux.	Where in my life am I constantly shifting?
Dust	Aridity. Potential for growth.	Where in my life have I withheld the flow of feeling?
Dwarf	The power of the small. Unconscious forces. Magic.	What am I working to transform?

Image:	Associations:	Ask Yourself:
Dynamite	Explosive force. Sudden change.	What is ready to blow?
Eagle	Far-sighted vision and power.	What must I understand to be powerful?
Ear *See also* Body parts.	Receptivity.	What am I open to? What am I ready to hear?
Earth *See also* Elements.	Matter. Being grounded through nature.	How am I connected to the physical world?
Earthquake	Soul shaking. Deep levels of change.	What part of me is being shaken up?
East	Beginnings. Ancient truth.	Where am I heading?
Eating	Sustenance. Satisfaction. Pleasure.	What part of myself do I nurture?
Eclipse	Darkening of the light.	What fears am I ready to behold?
Eel	Work on commitment. Slipperiness.	What threatens my freedom of movement?
Egg	Potential. Birth. Hopes. Wholeness.	What do I wish to develop?

Eight *See also* Numbers.	Eternity. Abundance. Power. Cosmic consciousness.	What am I willing to receive?
Electrician	Work on energy or life force.	What part of me needs a charge?
Electricity *See* Electrician.		
Elements *See subheadings.*		
—air	Breath. Intelligence. Force of mind.	What area of my life requires stimulation?
—earth	Matter. Being grounded through nature.	How am I connected to the physical world?
—fire	Spirit. Energy. Unpolluted and cleansing.	In what areas of my life do I seek to be inspired or renewed?
—water	Emotion. Dissolving. Yielding. Release. Cleansing.	What am I feeling?
Elephant *See also* Animals, wild.	Wisdom. Memory. The power of persistence.	Where does my wisdom lie?
Elevator	Ascension. Increased understanding.	What am I doing to get higher?

Image:	Associations:	Ask Yourself:
Eleven *See also* Numbers.	Inspiration. Revolution. Higher octave of two.	What am I ready to change?
Elf *See* Dwarf; Fairy.		
Embrace *See* Hugging.		
Embryo *See* Fetus.		
Emerald	Promise. Luxuriance.	What supports my growth?
Employment *See also* Job.	Occupation. Fulfillment.	What am I ready to do?
Empty	Containing nothing. Unloading.	What is gone? What do I want to get rid of?
Epilepsy *See* Seizures.		
Equator	Rite of passage. Movement from one sphere of activity to another.	How am I becoming more whole?

Erection	Creative power. Fertility.	What do I want to do or to make?
See also Sex.		
Eruption	Explosion of unconscious material.	What must I clear?
Escalator		
See Elevator.		
Eunuch	Cutting off sexuality.	How can I be safe and sexual?
See also Castration.		
Europe *or* European	Culture. Old World. Preservation of the past.	What do I wish to continue or to save?
Evergreen	Persistence in time. Unchanging.	What is eternal in me?
Exam		
See Test.		
Ex-boyfriend	Masculine ideal, either integrated or rejected.	What have I accepted or failed to accept within myself?
Excrement	Elimination. Garbage from the past.	What am I ready to forget?
Execute	Punishment. Judgment.	In what areas of my life am I ready to forgive myself?
See also Judge.		
Exercise	Flexibility. Strength. Stamina.	What new strengths do I want to take form? What am I building up?

91

Image:	Associations:	Ask Yourself:
Ex-girlfriend	Feminine ideal, either integrated or rejected.	What have I accepted or failed to accept within myself?
Exhaustion	Squandered energy. Depression. Debility.	What feelings do I wish to avoid? What do I prefer not to think about?
Exhibitionism *See also* Sex.	Exposure.	What part of myself do I need to see or to understand?
Ex-husband	Male aspect of self, either integrated or rejected.	What have I accepted or refused to accept within myself?
Explosion	Sudden, violent change.	What is ready to burst forth?
Extinct	No longer existing.	What part of me has been annihilated?
Extramarital sex *See also* Sex.	Illicit union.	What is lacking in my relationship with myself?
Ex-wife	Feminine aspect of self, either integrated or rejected.	What have I accepted or refused to accept within myself?
Eye *See also* Body parts.	Vision. Consciousness. Clarity.	What am I aware of? How do I see the world?

Eyelashes *See also* Body parts.	Protection of vision. Allure.	How well do I see? What can I safely observe? What do I show to the world?
Face *See also* Body parts.	Identity. Ego. Self-image.	How do I appear?
Face-lift	Repair of self-image. Renewal. Vanity.	What part of my identity is ready for a make-over?
Fairground	Wholesome recreation. Festivity. Recognition.	What am I celebrating? What am I recognizing?
Fairy	Elemental being. Nature spirit.	What realms beyond the ordinary do I wish to explore?
Fall (season)	Cycle of transformation. Results.	In what areas of my life am I ready to benefit from my past efforts?
Falling	Fear of failure. Loss of power. Loss of control.	Where in my life do I feel out of control? Where do I want to land?
False teeth *See* Body parts: *teeth.*		
Family	Kin. Group.	What am I ready to relate to? What do I feel part of?

93

Image:	Associations:	Ask Yourself:
Farm	Domestication of nature. Sustenance.	What do I want to provide for myself and others?
Farmer	Work on relationship to nature.	What do I nurture in myself?
Farting	Defensiveness. Passive aggression. Failure to digest experience.	Where in my life am I ready to be more direct?
Fat	Protection. Sensitivity. Safety.	What fears am I ready to lose?
Father	Authority. Control. Guidance. Recognition.	What do I take care of?
Faucet *See also* Water.	Control or release of emotion.	What feelings do I turn on and off?
Fax	Contraction of space-time.	What am I ready to communicate instantly?
Fear	Unexpressed love. Self-doubt.	What am I ready to accept in myself and others?
Feather	Effortlessness. Delicacy.	What is easy for me? What tickles my fancy?
Fence	Boundary. Separation. Where differences meet.	What am I fencing in or fencing out?

94

Fetus	Potential. Conceived but not yet brought to birth.	What do I wish to produce?
Field	Expanse. Area of activity.	What am I ready to cultivate in myself?
Fight	Violent resolution. Release of energy.	What conflict am I building or releasing?
File	Records. Organization.	What do I wish to keep in order?
Films	The script or story being acted out. A means of distancing from events.	What is my story? What do I want to observe?
Finding	Discovery. Realization.	What am I ready to possess?
Finger *See also* Body parts.	Sensitivity. Awareness.	What am I touching?
Fingernails *See also* Body parts.	Safe handling. Glamorous or functional.	What am I prepared to handle, or what do I wish to avoid doing?
Fire	Spirit. Energy. Unpolluted and cleansing.	In what areas of my life do I seek to be inspired, renewed?
Fireflies	Messages. Inspiration.	What quickens me to life?

95

Image:	Associations:	Ask Yourself:
Fireman	Protective masculine aspect of self.	What part of me needs to be rescued? What do I want to rescue?
Fireplace *See also* House.	Source of energy, heat, spiritual center of self.	What is central to me? What warms me?
Fish	Emotion. Freedom of movement in element of feeling. Inner self.	What do I feel?
Fishing *See also* Fish.	Seeking underneath or inside for nourishment.	What do I hope to catch?
Five *See also* Numbers.	Quintessence. Change. Celebration.	What is evolving in me?
Flag	Patriotism. Identification.	What am I loyal to?
Flame *See also* Fire.	Inspiration. Intensity of emotion.	What feelings am I compelled to express?
Flasher	Frustrated sexuality. Exhibitionism.	In what ways am I denying my sexual needs or urges?

Flea	Inescapable minor irritations.	What old troubles am I ready to deal with?
Flirtation	Affectation of love.	Where or with whom do I wish to be intimate?
Floating	Effortlessness. Buoyant.	What feelings support me?
Flood *See also* Water.	Overflow of emotion.	What feelings are too much for me?
Floor *See also* House.	Foundation. Basic elements.	Where in my life do I want to create stability?
Flower	Beauty. Sexuality. Blossoming.	In what ways are my beauty and sexuality blossoming?
Flying	Most common ecstatic dream. A joyous combination of control and freedom.	Where in my life do I feel this joyous power?
Flying fish *See also* Fish.	Freedom of feeling.	What experiences or emotions send me soaring?
Fog	Limited vision. Confusion.	Where in my life do I seek clarity?
Following	Pursuit.	What wants to be close to me? What am I ready to be close to?

Image:	Associations:	Ask Yourself:
Food	Nourishment. Security. Pleasure or greed.	What do I nourish in myself? What am I hungry for?
Foot *See also* Body parts.	Grounding. Direction. Basic beliefs.	Where am I going?
Football *See also* Ball game; Sports.		
Foreign *See also* Countries.	Distant. Strange. Exotic.	What is boring about my life?
Foreigner	Expansion of self into unfamiliar realms.	What am I ready to explore in myself?
Forest	The realm of the unconscious. Natural forces.	What part of my inner nature am I ready to explore?
Fort	Defended self.	What defenses am I ready to examine?
Foundation *See also* House.	Basic principles or beliefs. Grounding.	What am I ready to make solid or secure?
Foundling	Abandoned aspect of self.	What part of myself am I preparing to care for?

Fountain *See also* Water.	Emotion springing forth. Freedom of emotional expression. Release.	What feelings are welling up in me?
Four *See also* Numbers; Square.	Stability. Matter. Strength. Worldly effort.	Where in my life am I most stable?
Fox *See also* Animals, wild.	Cleverness. Cunning.	What do I trust, or not trust, in myself?
Freak	Abnormal. Unconventional.	What unique qualities am I ready to express?
Free *or* freedom	Independence. Release.	What part of myself am I ready to liberate?
Freeway	Travel. Route to freedom. Movement.	Where in my life am I free to move?
Freezer	Preserve. Chill.	What feelings are frozen within me?
Friend	Aspect of self ready for integration.	What part of me is being integrated?

Image:	Associations:	Ask Yourself:
Frog *See also* Animals, wild.	Transformation.	What beauty lies within me?
Frozen *See also* Water.	Preservation. Restraint.	What rigid feelings am I ready to dissolve?
Fruit	Product. Offspring.	What am I ready to harvest?
Frying pan *See also* Pan.	Tool or weapon. Basic equipment.	What do I provide? How am I getting down to basics?
Funeral	The end or death of something.	What part of me is ready to go?
Fun house	Amusement. Fear as pleasure.	What old frights am I beginning to find amusing?
Fur	Protection. Warmth. Luxury. Status.	What covers me?
Furniture *See also* House.	Identity. Attitudes. Beliefs.	How do I furnish the house of my self?
Gallery *See* Art gallery.		

Gambling	Reward. Hope of recognition.	Where in my life am I ready to win?
Gangster	Criminal. Rule of force.	What new rules do I want to establish for myself?
Garage *See also* House.	Storage. Protection.	How do I take care of my power?
Garbage	Cleaning and clearing up.	What am I ready to get rid of?
Garden	Inner self. Growth or blossoming.	What do I nurture in myself?
Gardener	Natural process. Growth.	What is growing in me?
Gay *See* Homosexual.		
Gear	Ideas. Attitudes. Beliefs.	What do I value? What is useful to me?
Ghost	Spiritual aspect of self—sometimes feared. Memory.	What keeps coming back for me?
Ghoul	Death in life.	What part of myself threatens my survival?

Image:	Associations:	Ask Yourself:
Gift	Recognition. Acknowledgment.	What part of myself do I wish to honor? What do I appreciate?
Giraffe *See also* Animals, wild.	Overview. Shy grace.	Where in my life am I ready to extend my vision?
Girl	Receptive or yin quality developing.	Where in my life am I learning to be receptive?
Girlfriend	Feminine ideal.	What do I admire in a female? What feminine aspect am I ready to integrate?
Glad *See* Joy.		
Glasses	Vision. Attitude. Belief.	What correction is necessary for me to see clearly?
Glue	Uniting. Repairing.	What is coming together for me?
Goat *See also* Animals, domestic.	Lusty vigor. Relentless energy. Omnivorous.	What am I determined to do?

102

Goblin	Apparition of fear.	What fears am I ready to examine or confront?
God	Divine masculine. Sacred. Creator.	What do I hold sacred?
Goddess	Divine feminine. Compassion. Love.	What qualities do I worship?
Gold	Ultimate value. Splendor.	What do I treasure? What part of me has great worth?
Goldfish *See also* Fish; Gold.	Low maintenance. Impermanence.	What small things give me pleasure?
Golf	High-status recreation.	How can I enjoy increased self-worth?
Goose *See also* Animals, domestic.	Silly, aggressive, watchful.	Am I silly? Where in my life is my aggression apt to break out?
Gorilla *See also* Animals, wild.	Strength. Innocence. Rarity.	In what areas of my life am I ready to be strong and gentle?
Government	Administrative regulation. Control. Provider.	Where in my life do I feel controlled or taken care of?
Grace	Blessing. Rapture.	What is transcendent within me?

103

Image:	Associations:	Ask Yourself:
Grandparent	Gentle authority. Kindness.	Where in my life do I seek support?
Grass	Natural protection. Ubiquity.	What part of myself can I always rely on?
Gravel *See also* Rock; Stone.	Utility. Common.	Where in my life am I ready to be practical?
Graveyard *See also* Cemetery; Garden.		
Gray *See also* Colors.	Transition from one state to another. If clear, peace. If dull, fear.	What am I moving toward?
Green *See also* Colors.	Growth. Serenity. Healing through growth.	Where in my life am I growing?
Groceries *See also* Food.	Nurture. Necessities.	What do I need to feel well supplied?
Grocery store	Source of provisions.	What am I ready to provide for myself?
Groom	Masculine activity and energy.	What union am I ready to commit myself to?

Guilt *or* guilty	Judgment.	What am I ready to forgive in myself or in others?
Guinea pig *See also* Animals, domestic.	Fecundity. Responsibleness.	What am I learning to care for?
Gulf	Abyss. Enclosing vastness.	What boundaries do I seek?
Gun	Violence. Aggression. Threat.	What threatens me? Where in my life do I want protection?
Guru	Knowledge. Inspiration. Obsession. Devotion.	How do I wish or fear to be more powerful in the world?
Guts *See also* Body parts.	Fortitude. Stamina.	From what source do I draw my strength?
Hair *See also* Body parts.	Protection. Attraction. Sensuality.	What am I covering? What do I display?
Hairdresser	Work on self-image and self-esteem.	What am I ready to feel better about?
Hall *See also* House.	Access. Privacy.	How well do the parts of myself connect?

105

Image:	Associations:	Ask Yourself:
Hammer	Construction. Striking out.	Where in my life am I building or tearing down?
Hamster *See also* Animals, domestic.	Dependency. Cuteness.	What part of me needs to be cared for?
Hand *See also* Body parts.	Capacity. Competence. Help.	What am I ready to handle?
Handbag *See* Clothing: *purse.*		
Handicapped *See* Disabled.		
Handle	Understanding. Usefulness.	What am I ready to make use of?
Hanging	Holding back communication.	What am I ready to say or hear?
Harbor *See also* Water.	Shelter. Safety.	Where in my life do I find emotional peace?
Hat *See also* Clothing.	Opinons. Thoughts.	What thoughts or attitudes do I reveal?

Haunted house *See also* House.	Childhood fears. Prohibition. Past limitation.	What part of my past am I ready to purify or exorcise?
Head *See also* Body parts.	Intellect. Understanding. Superior.	What am I ready to understand?
Healer *or* healing	Restoration. Recovery.	Where in my life am I ready to be whole?
Hearing aid	Work on failure to communicate.	What am I preparing to hear?
Heart *See also* Body parts.	Love. Security.	Where in my life am I ready to give and receive love?
Heart attack	Loss of love or security.	Where in my life do I need to give and receive more love?
Heat	Intense emotion. Stress.	Where do I need to cool off?
Heaven	Bliss. Transcendence.	Where in my life do I feel blessed?
Helicopter *See also* Vehicles.	Movement in many directions.	Where in my life do I want more freedom of movement?
Hell	Torment. Spiritual agony.	What am I ready to forgive in myself or others?

Image:	Associations:	Ask Yourself:
Helmet *See also* Clothing.	Protected opinions and attitudes.	What thoughts or opinions am I ready to change?
Herb	Savor. Subtlety.	In what way am I seeking more flavor from life?
Herd *See* Crowd.		
Herpes	Misuse of sexual energy. Unwise sexual expression.	What worries me about sex?
High heels *See also* Clothing.	Glamour. Restriction. Sexual invitation.	How comfortable am I with conventional femininity?
High places	Attainment. Greater understanding.	What do I want to achieve? Where must I go to achieve it?
High-rise *See* Skyscraper.		
High school *See* High places; School.		
Highway *See* High places; Road.		

Term	Meaning	Question
Hiking	Work on process. Advancement.	Where do I want to go? Am I strong enough to make it?
Hill	Easy achievement. Comfortable progress.	What is easy for me to do?
Hippie	Freedom. Excess. Rejection of conventional values.	What part of me desires or fears to be different?
Hippopotamus *See also* Animals, wild.	Vast strength. Hidden danger. Size.	How do I conceal my power?
Hitchhiker	Freedom. Irresponsibility.	What part of me wants a free ride?
Hologram	Totality. The part as equal to the whole.	In what way am I ready to see the perfection of my being?
Home *See also* House.	Center of being. Spiritual self.	Where does my spirit reside?
Homeless *See also* House.	Spiritual deprivation. Absence of security and stability.	What new structure am I seeking?
Homosexual *See also* Sex.	Union—or fear of union—with aspects of self.	What part of my femininity or masculinity do I seek to merge with?

Image:	Associations:	Ask Yourself:
Hook *See also* Fishing.	To ensnare. Trap.	What do I want to catch?
Hooker *See* Prostitute.		
Horse *See also* Animals, domestic; Vehicles.	Swift. Usually elegant. Feeling of developed consciousness. Sometimes unexpressed sexuality.	How do I feel about my power? What natural force am I suppressing or expressing?
Horse, flying *or* winged *See also* Animals, domestic.	Soaring consciousness. Limitless nature of self.	What part of me is ready to soar?
Hose *See also* Water.	Flexibility. Flow of emotion.	How well do I communicate my feelings?
Hospital	Healing. Confinement.	What am I ready to heal?
Hostage	Imprisonment as security.	What do I get from holding myself or others back?
Hot *See* Heat.		

Hotel	Transitional aspect of identity.	What part of me is in transit?
House *See also subheadings.*	Being. The house of self.	What do I believe or fear about myself?
—*apartment*	A part of the total house of self.	What part of myself do I occupy?
—*attic*	Higher consciousness. Memory. Stored-up past.	What is "up there" that I want or fear to explore?
—*basement*	Below. The unconscious.	What part of my unconscious is ready to be seen?
—*bathroom*	Place of cleansing and release.	What am I ready to release?
—*bedroom*	Privacy. Rest. Intimacy.	What is my inner reality?
—*castle*	Fortified but noble self.	What walls am I ready to remove?
—*ceiling*	Upper limits.	Where in my life am I ready to raise my limits?
—*cottage*	Cozy, familiar house of the self.	What part of me wants to be snug?
—*dining room*	The ritual of eating. Formality.	What sustenance do I require?
—*door*	Access. Movement from one area to another.	What space am I ready to enter or to keep private?

111

Image:	Associations:	Ask Yourself:
—*fireplace*	Source of energy, heat, spiritual center of self.	What is central to me? What warms me?
—*floor*	Foundation. Basic elements.	Where in my life do I want to create stability?
—*foundation*	Basic principles or beliefs. Grounding.	What am I ready to make solid or secure?
—*furniture*	Identity. Attitudes. Beliefs.	How do I furnish the house of my self?
—*garage*	Storage. Protection.	How do I take care of my power?
—*hall*	Access. Privacy.	How well do the parts of myself connect?
—*haunted house*	Childhood fears. Prohibition. Past limitation.	What part of my past am I ready to purify or exorcise?
—*home*	Center of being. Spiritual self.	Where does my spirit reside?
—*homeless*	Spiritual deprivation. Absence of security and stability.	What new structure am I seeking?
—*hut*	Basic or primordial needs. Retreat. Humility.	Where in my life am I ready to be humble?

112

—*kitchen*	Nourishment. Productivity.	What's cooking?
—*living room*	Central space of the house of self.	What is central to my being?
—*mansion*	Expansive residence of the self.	What part of me needs more room?
—*palace*	Potential kingdom of the self.	How can I fulfill my potential?
—*porch*	Intersection of self with the world.	Where in my life am I ready to be more approachable?
—*rafters*	Protective support.	What supports my higher consciousness?
—*roof*	Above. Protection. Covering.	Where in my life am I ready to expand my limitations?
—*stairs*	Ascent. Going higher. Aspiration. Descent. Grounding.	What do I want to rise or descend to?
—*wall*	Barrier. Defense. Partition.	What am I ready to integrate? What separation is necessary for me?
—*window*	Vision. Seeing and being seen.	What am I willing to see? What do I wish to reveal or conceal?

113

Image:	Associations:	Ask Yourself:
Hugging *See also* Sex.	Loving protection. Acknowledgment.	What part of me needs more attention?
Hunting	Pursuit. Search. Quest.	What part of my larger self am I ready to apprehend?
Hurricane	Destructive emotions.	What powerful feelings am I ready to experience?
Hurting	Work on old pains.	What wounds do I wish to heal?
Husband	Yang aspect of self. Partner.	What am I committed to?
Hut *See also* House.	Basic or primordial needs. Retreat. Humility.	Where in my life am I ready to be humble?
Hydrofoil *See also* Travel; Vehicles.	Soaring above the sea of feeling.	What emotions no longer inhibit me?
Hypodermic *See also* Injection.		
Ice *See also* Water.	A rigid feeling state. Frozen.	What feelings are locked within or ready to be melted away?

Ice pick — Cold feelings. — What feelings are frozen in me?

Ill *or* illness
See Sick.

Incest
See also Sex. — Fear of love. — Am I ready to be sexually mature?

Indian
See Native American.

Injury — Work on old wounds. — What damage am I ready to repair?

Injection — Forceful introduction. Need. — What must I have?

Insane
See Crazy.

Insect
See Bug.

Insurance — Absence of trust. Security. — What losses do I fear? How do I block my own progress?

Intercourse
See also Sex. — Union. Release. Pleasure. Creation. — What do I want or fear to merge with?

115

Image:	Associations:	Ask Yourself:
Intestines *See* Guts.		
Intoxication *See* Drunk.		
Invalid *See also* Cripple; Disabled.	Infirmity. Work on long-standing weakness or illness.	What old limitations am I ready to heal?
Invasion	Forced entry. Attack.	What part of me is ready to be more assertive?
Iron	Rigidity. Steadfastness. Endurance.	Where in my life must I stand firm?
Island	Solitude. Separation. Escape. May be enjoyable or lonely.	What do I separate myself from?
Jacket *See also* Clothing.	Freedom of movement. Adventure.	Where in my life do I seek liberty of action?
Jackhammer	Breaking up of old structures.	What course am I ready to change?

Jade | Protection. Good fortune. | Where in my life do I feel blessed or wish to be blessed?

Jail
See Prison.

Jaw
See also Body parts. | Will. Relentless anger. | Where in my life must I dominate? Where am I ready to yield?

Jealousy | Work on fear of intimacy. | Where in my life am I ready to show my vulnerability?

Jeep
See also Vehicle. | Ruggedness. Utility. Efficiency. | Where in my life must I be sturdy to reach my goal?

Jellyfish | Spineless. Passive aggression. | Where in my life am I ready to express myself more forcefully?

Jesus
See also Christ. | Human aspect of divinity. Salvation. Healing. | What part of me is ready to be saved?

Jewel | Treasure. Essence. Precious. | What is valuable? What do I value in myself?

Jewelry | Display. Wealth. Status. | What is my worth? How do I show it?

117

Image:	Associations:	Ask Yourself:
Job *See also* Employment.	Work on fulfillment.	Where in my life am I frustrated or satisfied?
Joint	Connection. Junction.	What is coming together for me?
Journey *See also* Travel.	Liberation. Movement toward inner center.	What is my inner process?
Joy	Gladness. Abundant well-being.	What have I accepted unconditionally?
Judge	Decision making. Wisdom or condemnation.	What decision am I ready to make? What part of me is wise and knowledgeable?
Junk *or* junkyard	Discarded ideas, attitudes, beliefs.	What value can I find in the past?
Key	Solution. Access.	What problem am I ready to solve?
Kidnapped	Work on independence and freedom.	What responsibilities do I wish or fear to assume?
Killing *See* Murder.		

118

King	Noble aspect of masculinity.	Where in my life am I ready to express masculine power?
Kissing *See also* Sex.	Intimacy. Affection. Greeting.	What or whom do I wish to be close to?
Kitchen *See also* House.	Nourishment. Productivity.	What's cooking?
Knee *See also* Body parts.	Flexibility. Humility.	Where in my life do I need to bend?
Knife	Aggression. Severing. Anger.	What do I want to cut out?
Knob	Protuberance.	What sticks out? What am I ready to notice?
Knot *See also* Knots.	Bond of union. Entanglement. Complication.	What is connected in me? What do I want or fear to tie together?
Knots *See also* Knot.	Restriction. Holding together.	What is tied up in me?
Ku Klux Klan	Secret terrorism. Prejudice.	What hidden fears or judgments am I preparing to confront?
Laboratory	Exploration. Detached examination.	What am I searching for?

119

Image:	Associations:	Ask Yourself:
Labyrinth *See* Maze.		
Ladder	Reaching upward.	How high am I ready to climb?
Lake *See also* Water.	Contained emotion. Often a sense of tranquillity or peace.	What feelings do I comfortably contain?
Lanai *See* Deck.		
Landslide	Work on emotional stability. Fear of change.	What old survival skills am I ready to drop?
Latino *or* Latina	Spontaneity. Relaxation. Volatility.	What do I wish to change? What part of me is impulsive?
Laughing	Communication of joy. Joyous release. Scorn.	In what way am I ready to lighten up? What pressure do I want to release?
Laundry *See also* Cleaning; Clothing.	Cleansing. Purification. Release.	What am I ready to clean up? What has been sullied through use?

Lawyer *See* Attorney.		
Leash	Control. Restraint.	What leads me? What am I attached to?
Lecturing	Communication. Sermonize.	What am I ready to hear or to say? What is my expertise?
Leg *See also* Body parts.	Support. Movement.	What supports me? Am I getting somewhere?
Lei *See also* Corsage.	Token of honor or affection.	What do I wish to recognize in myself?
Lesbian *See* Homosexual.		
Lever	Purchase. Take charge.	What do I want to maneuver?
Library	Knowledge. Records. Research. The past.	What does the past have to tell me?
Light	Illumination. Vision.	What am I ready to see?
Lighthouse	Self-illumination. Warning. Guidance.	What do I need to see to avoid danger?
Lightning	Flash of illumination. Sudden vision.	What is awakening in me?

121

Image:	Associations:	Ask Yourself:
Lightning bugs *See* Fireflies.		
Limousine *See also* Vehicles.	Luxurious power. Extravagance.	Where in my life am I ready to be conspicuous in my expression of power?
Limping	Work on freedom of movement. One-sidedness.	What balance am I seeking? Which side am I developing?
Lion *See also* Animals, wild.	Nobility. Strength. Pride.	Where does courage dwell in me?
Little	Smaller than usual. Reduced. Insignificant.	Where in my life do I feel diminished? What am I ready to reduce?
Liver	Bad feelings. Sluggishness.	What peace am I seeking? In what way am I ready to be compassionate?
Living room *See also* House.	Central space of the house of self.	What is central to my being?

Lizard *See also* Animals, wild.	Cold-blooded. Reptilian.	Where in my life am I ready to show more warmth?
Load	Encumbrance. Burden.	What am I ready to put down? Where in my life do I want to lighten up?
Lobby	Public space.	What am I willing to make known?
Lock	Security. Confinement.	What am I ready to open up or close away?
Locker *See also* School.	Storage. Safekeeping.	What have I stored away? What am I ready to remember?
Lost	Without direction. Missing.	Where in my life am I lacking in confidence?
Lottery *See also* Gambling.	Chance. Good fortune. Risk.	Where in my life do I look for a large benefit at little cost?
Love affair *See* Affair.		
Lover	The idealized inner self. Anima. Animus.	What part of my larger self is ready to be integrated?

123

Image:	Associations:	Ask Yourself:
Luggage *See also* Baggage.	Belongings. Beliefs.	What am I taking with me? What am I ready to leave behind?
Lumber *See also* Wood.	Supplies for growth.	What am I building or constructing?
Lungs *See also* Body parts.	Breath of life. Freedom.	In what ways is my life ready to expand?
Lust *See also* Sex.	Eagerness for possession.	What will satisfy me? Where in my life am I unfulfilled?
Machine	Automation. Convenience. Repetition.	What burdensome work am I ready to be free of?
Mad *See* Crazy; Rage.		
Magazine	Stimulation. Consumption.	Where in my life are my desires unrealized?
Maggot *See* Worm.		
Magician	Work on command of inner and outer worlds or forces. Transformation.	What powers do I control or fear?

Mail	News. Guidance.	What do I want to hear or learn?
Mail carrier	Work on communication.	What do I want to hear or say?
Makeup	Image. Feminine projection.	Who do I show to the world?
Mall	Central resources. Community. Consumption.	What needs or desires do I share with others?
Man	Yang aspect. Active.	Where in my life am I ready to be more assertive?
Manager	Work on organization.	How am I ready to be more efficient?
Mandala	The totality of the self. Wholeness.	Where in my life am I ready to express my totality of being?
Mansion See also House.	Expansive residence of the self.	What part of me needs more room?
Map	Guidance. Directions.	What information do I need to make my journey?
Marriage	Union. Commitment.	What am I ready to join or commit myself to?
Martial arts	Disciplined strength or force.	How am I refining my power?

Image:	Associations:	Ask Yourself:
Mask	Disguise. Persona. Attitudes.	What do I hide? What do I display?
Masquerade *See* Disguise.		
Masturbation *See also* Sex.	Self-love.	What part of myself am I ready to accept and love?
Maze	Puzzle. Labyrinth.	What intricate problems am I ready to solve?
Meat	Essential nourishment. Sometimes a need to survive.	What must I do to survive? Where am I ready to trust?
Mechanic	Repair. Make good. Work on what has been damaged.	What damage am I ready to restore?
Medicine	Healing. Antidote.	Where in my life am I ready to be healthy and whole?
Melting *See also* Water.	Letting go.	What old structures am I ready to dissolve?
Menstruation	Power or fear of feminine identity.	Where am I ready to express more natural power?

Mercury	Liveliness. Inconstancy.	What part of me seeks stability? Where in my life do I feel stuck?
Mermaid *or* merman	Emotional part of identity.	What do I want to feel?
Merry-go-round	Innocent fun. Mindless repetition.	What simple pleasures satisfy me? Do I feel trapped by circumstances?
Metal	Endurance. Rigidity. Resolution.	Where in my life must I stand firm?
Microphone	Communication.	Where in my life am I ready to speak out?
Microwave	Accelerated processing.	What am I in a hurry for?
Military	Work on aggression.	Where in my life am I threatened? What strengthens me?
Milk *See also* Food.	Maternal love. Sustenance. Kindness.	What part of me is developing and seeks nourishment?
Minister	Work on compassion or care giving.	Where in my life am I ready to be more understanding?

Image:	Associations:	Ask Yourself:
Minotaur	Union of beastly and human nature.	Where in my life is blind impulse a threat to me?
Miracle	Supernatural wonder.	Where in my life do I feel the perfection of my own being?
Mirror	Image. Identity.	What part of me is reflected? What am I ready to see?
Mist *See also* Water.	Delicate expanse of feeling. Cool and comfortable.	What emotional field surrounds me?
Mob *See also* Crowd.	Loss of organizing principle or control.	Where in my life am I ready to command my conflicting desires?
Mobile phone *See* Car; Cellular phone; Telephone.		
Monastery	Spiritual community. Withdrawal from worldly affairs.	Where in my life do I seek to join with my spiritual peers?
Money	Security. Riches.	What do I value?

Monk	Retreat. Spiritual life.	What part of me needs to withdraw from life's demands?
Monkey *See also* Animals, wild.	Dexterity. Mischief. Humor.	What part of me is almost human?
Monster	Denied self. Threat.	What do I fear in myself?
Monument	Work on worthiness or recognition.	What do I value in myself? How do I wish to be remembered?
Moon	Emotion. Reflection. Inner self.	What feelings do I reflect?
Moss	Stillness. Slow growth.	Where in my life am I ready to be more patient?
Motel *See* Hotel.		
Mother	Nurturance. Approval or disapproval.	What do I care for in myself?
Motorcycle *See also* Vehicles.	Virility. Vigor. Display.	How hot am I? Where in my life am I ready to be more masterful?
Mountain	Aspiration. Success through effort.	What am I ready to achieve?

129

Image:	Associations:	Ask Yourself:
Mouse *See also* Animals, wild.	Meek nature. Quiet. Minor problems. Inner feelings. Shyness.	What small troubles are gnawing away at me?
Mouth *See also* Body parts.	Nourishment. New attitudes.	What am I ready to take in? What am I ready to express?
Movies *See* Films.		
Movie star	Glamour. Recognition. Fame.	What part of me is ready to be in the spotlight?
Moving	New life. A fresh start.	What lies ahead for me? What am I ready to leave behind?
Mud *See also* Water.	Messy feelings. Fertility. Stuck.	What emotions am I ready to clean up? What is growing?
Mule *See also* Animals, domestic.	Obstinate. Intractable. Stamina.	Where in my life am I ready to persevere?
Mummy	Reverence for the past. Ancient wisdom.	What do I wish to preserve or remember? What endures in me?

130

Murder	Violent completion.	What will I do anything to end?
Muscles *See also* Body parts.	Power. Strength.	In what aspects of my life am I ready to be more powerful?
Music	Harmony. Expression.	What am I integrating?
Naked	Exposed. Vulnerable.	Where am I ready to be seen?
Nap *See also* Dreaming; Sleeping.	Relaxation and rest. Ease.	What part of me needs to take it easy?
Native	Intuitive self. Harmony with nature. Primordial being.	Where in my life do I seek alignment with nature?
Native American	Stoicism. Natural wisdom. Cunning.	What is untamed in me? Where in my life do I want more freedom from control?
Nausea *See* Seasick; Vomit.		
Navy	Command of feeling. Sometimes homosexual undertones.	What emotions am I ready to command?
Nazi	Totalitarian control. Sentimentality.	What extreme reactions am I ready to adjust?

131

Image:	Associations:	Ask Yourself:
Neck *See also* Body parts.	Flexibility, especially of vision.	What can I see if I make a small adjustment?
Necklace *See also* Jewelry.	Display. Distinction.	What am I proud of? What do I value in myself?
Needle	Piercing.	Where in my life am I ready to get the point? What do I wish to penetrate?
Neighbor	Fellowship.	What is close to me? What do I like or fear about myself?
Neighborhood	Work on community.	Where in my life am I ready to join with others?
Nerd	Insignificant but smart. Absence of charm.	Where in my life am I ready to be as attractive as I am smart?
Nest	Safety. Comfort.	Where in my life do I seek protection? What comforts me?
Nets	Safety. Entrapment.	Where in my life am I ready to be fearless?

Night	Mystery. Unconscious contents. Inner vision.	What darkness am I ready to penetrate?
Nightclub *See also* Night.	Stimulation. Entertainment.	What excitement do I seek?
Nightgown *See* Clothing: *dress*; Night.		
Nine *See also* Numbers.	Hidden blessings. Completion. Compassion.	What is revealed to me?
North	Death and transformation. Effort.	What do I want to end whatever the cost?
North Pole	Point of transformation. End of the journey.	What is over or complete for me?
Nose *See also* Body parts.	Instinctive knowledge.	How does it smell to me? What do I know without knowing?
Nuclear bomb *See* Atom bomb.		
Nude *See* Naked.		

Image:	Associations:	Ask Yourself:
Numbers *See subheadings.*	We lack a consistent cultural tradition for the interpretation of numbers. If a number appears repeatedly in a dream, or if it is highlighted, first ask yourself what personal significance it has for you. It may refer to an important date in your life, to a well-remembered address or birth date, or to other events or experiences. Begin by identifying these personal associations. Below is a common interpretation of numbers one through ten, with the addition of numbers eleven, twenty-two, and thirty-three. Dream consciousness is always hungry for new material; this system can easily be digested if you find it nourishing.	
—one	Beginning. Oneness. Essence. Individual will.	Who am I?
—two	Duality. Opposition. Balance. Partnership.	How do I relate?
—three	Trinity. Balance of opposites. Sociability.	How do I integrate my differences?
—four	Stability. Matter. Potential for sudden change. Worldly effort.	Where in my life am I most stable?
—five	Quintessence. Change. Celebration.	What is evolving in me?
—six	Expansion. Organization. Harmony. Domesticity.	What am I ready to commit to?
—seven	Energy given form. Cycles of growth. Discipline.	What am I ready to learn?

—*eight*	Eternity. Abundance. Power. Cosmic consciousness.	What am I willing to receive?
—*nine*	Hidden blessings. Completion. Compassion.	What is revealed to me?
—*ten*	New beginning on a higher octave.	What have I learned?
—*eleven*	Inspiration. Revolution. Higher octave of two.	What am I ready to change?
—*twenty-two*	Earthly mission. Self and others.	What do I trust?
—*thirty-three*	Salvation and temptation.	Where in my life have I succeeded or failed?
Nun	Retreat. Spiritual life.	What part of me needs to withdraw from life's demands?
Nurse	Healing care. Compassion.	What part of me needs to be cared for, or needs to care for others?
Nut	Essence. Kernel. Richness.	What is essential to my nourishment?
Oasis	Place of refuge and relaxation.	Where in my life do I seek a sanctuary?

135

Image:	Associations:	Ask Yourself:
Ocean *See also* Water.	Vast, limitless feeling. Sometimes an overwhelming emotion. Rich with abundant life.	What part of me relates to such vastness?
Octopus	Shy. Grasping.	What do I need to hold on to?
Odor *See* Smell.		
Office	Workplace. Professional aspect of self.	What am I working on or with?
Oil	Lubricity. Slipperiness.	What do I want to get unstuck? Where do I seek more freedom of movement?
Oily	Smarminess. Fawning.	Where in my life am I ready to be more direct?
Old	Maturity. Degeneration.	What is complete for me? What am I ready to replace?
One *See also* Numbers.	Beginning. Oneness. Essence. Individual will.	Who am I?
Ooze *See* Slime.		

Open	Opportunity. Potential.	What choice am I ready to make?
Opera	Elaborate or complex form. Epic.	What grandeur do I seek in my life?
Operation *See* Surgery.		
Opossum *See also* Animals, wild.	Feigning death.	What threatens me? Where am I ready to come to life?
Oracle	Prophecy. Ambiguity. Riddle.	What is becoming clear to me? What can I successfully decipher?
Oral sex *See also* Sex.	Gratification. Pleasure.	What part of me wants to give or receive gratification?
Orange *See also* Colors.	Emotion. Stimulation. Healing.	What am I feeling?
Orchid	Exotic glamour.	What is uniquely beautiful in me? How am I different from others?
Orgasm *See also* Sex.	Consummation.	What is complete for me?

137

Image:	Associations:	Ask Yourself:
Orgy *See also* Sex.	Indiscriminate union.	Where in my life am I ready to experience the oneness of all?
Oriental *See also* East.	Eastern wisdom. Subtlety.	Where in my life is wisdom developing for me?
Orphan	Lack of protection. Isolation.	What deep connections am I preparing to make?
Ostrich	Denial. Grounded.	What am I ready to deal with? What freedom do I seek?
Outer space *See also* Rocket; Spaceship.	Transcendence of personal reality.	What larger being do I seek to experience?
Outlaw	Rebellion. Adventure.	What freedom do I seek?
Overalls *See also* Clothing.	Common. Sturdiness. Protection.	What do I cover? What work is hard for me?
Owl	Wisdom. Vision.	What part of me is naturally wise?

Ox
See also Animals, domestic.
Burden. Strength. Stupidity.
How do I doubt my own strength? What makes me feel stupid?

Oyster
See also Food.
Tender inside, hard outside. Sexual stimulation.
What am I hungry for?

Pack
Load. Burden. Equipment.
What do I carry with me?

Package
Expectation. Mystery.
What am I looking for? What do I fear to find?

Packing
Preparation for movement. Sorting or storing old ideas.
What do I want to take or leave behind?

Pager
Accessibility. Availability.
What part of me is always on call?

Pain
Conflict. Problem. Suffering.
What hurts me? What parts of my self are denied?

Painting
See also Art; Artist.
Transforming. Decorating.
What do I wish to change or improve?

Palace
See also House.
Potential kingdom of the self.
How can I fulfill my potential?

139

Image:	Associations:	Ask Yourself:
Pan *See also* Satyr.	Divinity of nature. Unleashing.	What elemental aspects of my nature am I coming to terms with?
Pan (cooking utensil)	Basic equipment. Utensil.	What am I ready to prepare?
Panther *See also* Animals, wild.	Wild beauty. Grace.	What force do I wish or fear to unleash?
Panties *See also* Clothing.	Private self. Sexual identity.	What are my hidden feelings? What am I ready to expose?
Pants *See* Trousers.		
Panty hose *See* Tights.		
Parachute	Rescue. Deliverance.	What am I escaping from? Where do I want to land?
Parade	Fanciful display. Options.	What part of me wants to be seen?

Paradise *See* Heaven.		
Paralysis	Resistance. No change or growth.	What move am I preparing to make?
Paranoia	Work on obsessive fear.	What inner strength am I ready to recognize?
Parasite	Work on independence.	Where am I ready to fend for myself?
Paratrooper	Invasion The thrill of physical danger.	What territory do I want to encounter?
Parrot	Imitative. Humorous. Exotic.	Where in my life do I lack originality?
Party	Celebration. Festivity.	What am I ready to celebrate?
Passport	Freedom of movement. Identity.	What part of me wants to expand and explore?
Pastry *See also* Cake.	Luxury. Indulgence. Sweetness.	What do I crave? Is there enough sweetness in my life?
Path	Life's direction.	What do I feel about my chosen route?

141

Image:	Associations:	Ask Yourself:
Patio *See* Deck.		
Pattern	Established order.	What beliefs am I examining?
Paw *See also* Animals, domestic; Animals, wild.	Handling animal instincts.	Where in my life am I ready to trust my intuition?
Peacock	Pride and vanity. Display.	What do I wish to have seen or admired?
Peak *See also* Mountain.	Point of success. Achievement.	What am I heading for?
Peanut *See* Nut.		
Pearl *See also* Jewel.	Purity. Treasure. Transforming irritation to beauty.	What do I value? How is it created?
Pebbles	Serenity. Compactness.	What is coming together for me? What edges have been smoothed away?

142

Pedestal   Support. Inflation. Display. Admiration.   What do I wish or fear to show off? What do I look up to?

Pee *or* peeing
  See Urinating.

Peeping Tom
  See Voyeurism.

Penis   Male sexuality. Yang power.   How is my power expressed?
  See also Body parts.

Performing   Accomplishment. Achievement.   Where in my life do I seek recognition?

Perfume   Luxury. Indulgence. Balm.   What gratifies me? Where in my life do I seek more pleasure?

Period
  See Menstruation.

Pet   Work on self-love.   What part of myself do I care for?
  See also Animals, domestic.

143

Image:	Associations:	Ask Yourself:
Pharaoh	Absolute authority. Union of human with divinity.	What form of authority do I fear or trust in myself?
Phoenix	Rebirth. Renewal. Immortality.	What part of me cannot die?
Photograph	Image. Vision. Memory.	What do I remember? How do I see the world?
Photographer *See also* Camera.	Work on world image.	What image of the world do I want to preserve?
Picnic	Lighthearted nourishment.	Where in my life am I ready to be more carefree?
Picture *See* Painting; Photograph.		
Pig *See also* Animals, domestic.	Greedy. Smart. Sometimes slovenly, sometimes fastidious.	Am I grabbing more than I need or can use? Do I clean up my own mess?
Pigeon *See also* Bird.	Victimhood.	Where in my life am I ready to stand up for myself?
Pill	Aid. Relief. Medicine.	What do I need to feel better?

144

Pillow	Comfort. Intimacy.	What part of me seeks encouragement?
Pilot	Work on freedom of movement and change.	What destination am I hurrying towards?
Pimples	Ugliness. Small bursts of anger.	How am I ready to be less sensitive?
Pink *See also* Colors.	Affection. Love.	To what am I responding?
Pirate	Outlaw. Rejection of social rules and obligations.	What rules do I reject? Where do I feel restricted by society?
Plague	Universal disorder or disease.	What system do I believe is breaking down?
Plane *See also* Vehicles.	Rapid movement across great distance.	Am I in a hurry for change?
Planets	Cosmic harmony and influence. Celestial order.	Am I in or out of harmony with heavenly power?
Plants	Nature. Natural process. Fertility.	What is growing in me?
Plastic	Artificiality. Cheap substitute. Resilience.	What is the real thing?
Platform	Position. Stage.	What do I want to present?

Image:	Associations:	Ask Yourself:
Play	Performance. Script or production of life.	What changes in my life script am I considering?
Playing	Carefreeness. Joy.	Where in my life do I want more fun?
Playsuit *See also* Clothing.	Child aspect of self.	Where in my life do I want more enjoyment?
Plumber *or* plumbing	Work on emotional release.	What part of me needs clearing out or replacing?
Poetry	Quintessence of meaning.	What is essential for me?
Poison	Destructive actions or thoughts.	What no longer nourishes me?
Police	Work on order or control.	Where in my life do I seek order or fear control?
Politician	Work on policy. Choosing sides. Manipulation.	What side am I on? Where do I want to win?
Poor	Limited expression of resources.	What am I ready to develop?
Porch *See also* House.	Intersection of self with the world.	Where in my life am I ready to be more approachable?

146

Pornography
See also Sex.

Work on intimacy. Anonymous sex.

What part of myself am I afraid of exposing?

Porpoise
See Dolphin.

Possum
See Opossum.

Pottery
See Dishes.

Praying

Communion. Seeking help.

Where in my life am I ready to surrender?

Pregnancy

New life. Fecundity.

What am I preparing to produce?

Premature ejaculation
See also Sex.

Bad timing. Loss of control.

What feelings overwhelm me?

Present
See Gift.

President

Leadership or lack of leadership.

Where in my life am I ready or reluctant to lead?

147

Image:	Associations:	Ask Yourself:
Priest	Work on spiritual or religious well-being. Release.	What am I ready to forgive?
Prince	Noble aspect of self. Refined masculinity.	What do I admire or seek in men, or in myself?
Princess	Noble aspect of self. Refined feminity.	What do I admire to seek in women, or in myself?
Prison	Punishment. Confinement.	Where have I done wrong?
Procession *See also* Parade.	Ceremonial march. Pomp.	What beliefs am I ready to formalize or observe?
Project	Goal. Purpose.	What am I ready to accomplish?
Prostitute	If negative, misuse of sexuality. If positive, sexual healing.	What do I need to feel sexually healthy?
Pruning	Elimination of old growth.	What old stuff am I ready to cut away?
Psychic	Work on intuition, expanded consciousness.	In what way do I seek limitless awareness?

148

Psychokinesis	Power of consciousness over matter.	In what ways am I ready to take control of the world?
Pub *See* Tavern.		
Puddle *See also* Water.	Small but messy emotions.	What minor discomfort am I feeling?
Pulley	Movement with minimal effort.	What is easy for me to shift?
Punks	Alienation. Protest.	What part of me wants more love and attention?
Purple *See* Violet.		
Purse *See also* Clothing.	Feminine self. Sometimes sexual identity. Security.	What am I holding onto? What part of myself do I value?
Pursuit	Denied power.	What part of myself frightens me? Where can my strength be expressed safely?
Pyramid	Communication with greater consciousness. Ancient knowledge.	What height of awareness am I seeking?

Image:	Associations:	Ask Yourself:
Queen	Noble aspect of femininity.	Where in my life am I ready to express feminine power?
Quest *See also* Searching.	Adventure. Soul seeking.	What part of me holds the answer?
Quicksand	Insecurity. Instability.	Where in my life do I want a stronger foundation?
Rabbit *See also* Animals, wild; Animals, domestic.	Fertility. Luck. Insecurity.	Where in my life am I ready to be productive?
Race	Contest. Rivalry.	What is my goal? What am I missing by being in a hurry?
Radio	Story about reality. Communication.	What am I ready to hear or say?
Rafters *See also* House.	Protective support.	What supports my higher consciousness?
Rage	Work on victimhood.	What inner strength am I searching for?

Railroad
  See Train.

Rain
  See also Water.
Release of emotion. May be gentle and nourishing or dramatically threatening.
What feelings are pouring down on me?

Rainbow
Promise. Visible blessing.
What encourages me? Where do I expect to find happiness?

Rape
  See also Sex.
Forced union.
What do I fear being forced to unite with?

Rapids
  See also Water.
Active, stimulating emotions.
How comfortable am I with intense feelings?

Rapist
  See also Sex.
Forcing union.
Where in my life do I feel my love is rejected?

Rash
Irritations. Incidental anger.
How does caution restrict me? Am I too impetuous?

Rat
  See also Animals, wild.
Street smarts. Clever. Sneaky and untrustworthy.
Where in my life do I fear betrayal? Can I trust myself?

Raven
Magic. Omen. Sagacity.
What is the message?

151

Image:	Associations:	Ask Yourself:
Ravine *See* Canyon; Valley.		
Razor	Keen. Sharpness. Edge.	What do I want to cut off or make smooth?
Reading *See also* Book; Bookstore.	Exploring alternate realities or escape from present.	What worlds lie within me? What burdens me?
Recipe	Formula. Pattern.	What am I learning to do or make?
Red *See also* Colors.	Energy. Vigor. Passion.	What is my source of energy or strength?
Redhead *See also* Blond; Brunette.	Tempestuous. Dramatic. Spontaneous.	Where in my life do I want more vitality?
Reef *See also* Water.	Danger or safety of hidden emotions.	What underlies my feelings?
Refrigerator	Chilling to preserve.	What do I want to save?

152

Relatives	Unrecognized aspects of self.	What parts of my being am I ready to acknowledge?
Relocating *See* Moving.		
Remodeling *See also* House.	Restructuring the house of self.	What part of me needs more room or renewal? How do I want to appear to the world?
Repairing	Work on what has been damaged.	What am I ready to fix?
Restaurant	Place of nourishment. Choices.	What do I want to order?
Retarded	Work on development and training or education.	Where in my life do I want to catch up with others? Where do I fear being behind?
Reunion	Meeting with unrecognized aspects of self.	What part of my past am I ready to remember?
Rhinestone	Imitation. Cheap substitute.	Where in my life am I ready for the real thing?
Rhinoceros *See also* Animals, wild.	Blind strength. Armoring.	What am I ready to see or understand about my power?

153

Image:	Associations:	Ask Yourself:
Rich *or* riches	Worth. Security.	What do I wish or fear to possess?
Ring	Pledge. Commitment. Promise.	What union do I seek?
Riot *See also* Mob.	Loss of individuality. Destructive conformity.	Where in my life am I ready to stand alone?
River *See also* Water.	Flowing and active. May include dangerous rapids; may be smooth and tranquil.	What feelings are actively moving within me?
Road	Direction. Life's path.	Where am I going?
Robbery *See* Theft.		
Robot	Mechanical aspect of self.	What freedom do I seek?
Rock *See also* Stone.	Immutability. Security.	What do I want to make permanent?
Rocket *See also* Outer space; Spaceship.	Breaking free of physical limits. Exploration of inner space.	What limitations am I ready to transcend?

Rodeo	Exhibition of skill. Human control of animal force.	Where am I ready to display my skill at mastering wild forces?
Roller blades	Rapid movement with ease. Thrills.	What new freedom excites me?
Roller coaster	Ups and downs. Thrills. Wild but safe ride.	What excitement do I crave?
Roof *See also* House.	Above. Protection. Covering.	Where in my life am I ready to expand my limitations?
Rooster	Aggressive masculinity. Conceit.	What do I want to crow about?
Roots	Grounding. Nourishment.	What connects me to my source?
Rope	Connecting. Restraint.	What do I wish to join together or to control?
Rosary	Devotion. Piety.	What do I worship?
Rose	Goodness. Wholeness. Integration.	What is coming together within me?
Rubble *See* Debris.		
Ruby	Passionate awareness. Intensity. Sacred blood.	What do I care deeply about?
Rug *See* Carpet		

155

Image:	Associations:	Ask Yourself:
Running	Rapid movement. Escape. Joy of the physical.	What moves me?
R.V. *See also* Vehicles.	The joy of power. Rugged amusement.	Where in my life am I ready to enjoy the expression of power?
Sad *See also* Sorrow.		
Sadomasochism *See also* Sex.	Control of passion or instinct.	How does pain make me feel in control?
Sage	Work on wisdom or understanding.	Where in my life do I want to apply thought and good judgment?
Sailor *See also* Navy.	Navigating emotional seas.	What feelings am I taking charge of?
Sale	Good value. Opportunity.	What am I seeking that I fear I can't afford?
Salesperson *See also* Shopping.	Service. Availability.	What do I want to include in my life?

156

Salt	Savor. Flavor. Intensification.	What do I want to enhance in my life?
Samurai	Work on allegiance. Honor.	What am I committed to? Do my obligations limit me?
Sand	Barrenness. Immeasurability.	What is eternal in me? What prevents my growth?
Sandbox	Playful construction.	What new forms am I taking too seriously?
Sand dune *See* Dune.		
Sandpaper	Abrasiveness.	What roughness do I want to rub away?
Santa Claus	Belief. Getting what you want.	What do I believe I want?
Satellite	Message. Expansion through technology.	What distant news am I ready to hear?
Satyr *See also* Goat; Man.	Work on union of intellect with animal passion.	Where in my life am I integrating my mind and my body? Where do I seek sexual freedom?

157

Image:	Associations:	Ask Yourself:
Saw	Severing. Separation.	What am I forming?
Scalp *See* Body parts: *skin, hair.*		
Scar	Healed wound. Incomplete release of emotional hurt.	What am I ready to heal completely?
School	Education. Discipline.	What do I need to learn? What have I already learned and no longer need to study?
Scientist	Work on understanding or knowledge.	What do I want to comprehend or describe?
Scissors	Feminine weapon. Separation.	What do I wish to cut out?
Scorpion	Destructive feelings, thoughts, words.	Where in my life am I ready to express my authority and power?
Screw	Strong connection.	What am I joining together?
Screwdriver	Work on connection.	What am I preparing to connect?

158

Sea
See Ocean; Water.

Seal
See also Animals, wild.
Comic instinct. Playfulness.
Where do I seek more joy in life?

Sea lion
See Walrus.

Searching
See also Quest.
Recognition of desire or wants. Acknowledgment of need.
What am I finally ready to find?

Seashell
See Shell.

Seasick
Sickening emotions.
What feelings am I ready to get rid of?

Seat belt
See also Vehicles.
Safety Restraint.
What holds my power in check?

Seaweed
Growth within emotion. Can be nourishing or strangling.
What is developing in my sea of feeling?

Secondhand
Cheap. Serviceable.
Where in my life am I willing to make do or what am I willing to be satisfied by?

159

Image:	Associations:	Ask Yourself:
Secret	Work on what is hidden.	What am I ready to expose or uncover?
Secretary	Organization. Order. Help.	Where in my life do I need to get organized?
Security guard	Work on safety.	What part of me needs protection?
Security system	Safety insurance.	What defenses am I preparing to dismantle?
Sedative	Forgetfulness. Escape.	What is too stimulating or demanding for me?
Seed	Beginning. Source of greater being.	What or where do I wish to develop?
Seeking *See* Searching.		
Seizures	Extreme agitation. Spasmodic movement.	Where in my life do I fear or seek control?
Self-defense	Work on anger.	What inner strength do I seek?

Self-immolation	Burning pain.	What must I destroy in order to feel alive?
Semen *See also* Sex.	Yang aspect of fertility. Potency.	What am I bringing into being?
Senile	Work on declining abilities.	What is no longer important to me?
Serpent *See* Snake.		
Seven *See also* Numbers.	Energy given form. Cycles of growth. Discipline.	What am I ready to learn?
Sewer	Accumulation of negativity. Release.	What junk am I ready to get rid of?
Sewing	Joining together. Repair.	What do I want to create or restore?
Sex *See subheadings*.		
—*affair*	Surrender. Ardor.	What do I wish to yield to?
—*anal*	Submission. Union without issue.	To what or to whom do I want or fear to yield?

161

Image:	Associations:	Ask Yourself:
—arousal	Stimulation. Availability.	What do I want to respond to?
—bestiality	Union with animal passions or instincts.	What basic aspects of myself do I fear or deny?
—erection	Creative power. Fertility.	What do I want to do or to make?
—exhibitionism	Exposure.	What part of myself do I need to see or to understand?
—extramarital	Illicit union.	What is lacking in my relationship with myself?
—homosexual	Union—or fear of union—with aspects of self.	What part of my femininity or masculinity do I seek to merge with?
—hugging	Loving protection. Acknowledgment.	What part of me needs more attention?
—incest	Fear of love.	Am I ready to be sexually mature?
—intercourse	Union. Release. Pleasure. Creation.	What do I want or fear to merge with?

162

—kissing	Intimacy. Affection. Greeting.	What or whom do I wish to be close to?
—lust	Eagerness for possession.	What will satisfy me? Where in my life am I unfulfilled?
—masturbation	Self-love.	What part of myself am I ready to love and accept?
—oral	Gratification. Pleasure.	What part of me wants to give or receive gratification?
—orgasm	Consummation.	What is complete for me?
—orgy	Indiscriminate union.	Where in my life am I ready to experience the oneness of all?
—pornography	Work on intimacy. Anonymous sex.	What part of myself am I afraid of exposing?
—premature ejaculation	Bad timing. Loss of control.	What feelings overwhelm me?
—rape	Forced union.	What do I fear being forced to unite with?
—rapist	Forcing union.	Where in my life do I feel my love is rejected?

163

Image:	Associations:	Ask Yourself:
—*sadomasochism*	Control of passion or instinct.	How does pain make me feel in control?
—*semen*	Yang aspect of fertility. Potency.	What am I bringing into being?
—*voyeurism*	Safe distance from desires.	What do I want or fear to be close to?
Shadow	Hidden. Dark side of image.	What am I ready to illuminate?
Shaman	Manipulation of reality.	What part of my world am I transforming?
Shampoo *See* Hair; Soap.		
Shark	Dangers lurking in emotion.	What powerful feeling is threatening me?
Sheep *See also* Animals, domestic.	Conformity.	What am I following?
Shell	Protection. Can be limiting or covering. Beauty of form.	Which feelings do I need to protect? What structures do I value?

Shield
Protection. Security. Defense.
Where in my life am I ready to be more vulnerable?

Shipwreck
See also Boat; Wreck.

Shirt
See also Clothing.
Upper, as opposed to lower, self. Emotions.
What feelings do I consider appropriate?

Shit
See Excrement.

Shock
Sudden awakening. Illumination.
What arouses me? What awareness electrifies me?

Shoes
See also Clothing.
General situation. Grounding.
How well do I connect with the world?

Shooting
Destroying aspects of self.
What do I want to get rid of?

Shopping
Finding what you want. Options.
What am I ready to take home?

Shorts
See also Clothing.
Private self. Sexual identity.
What are my hidden feelings? What am I ready to expose?

Shotgun
See also Gun.
Widespread violence.
What damage is spreading around me?

Image:	Associations:	Ask Yourself:
Shoulders *See also* Body parts.	Strength or burdens.	What am I ready to carry? What is too heavy for me?
Shovel	Unearthing. Planting.	What am I digging up?
Shower	Cleansing. Release down the drain.	What do I want to wash away?
Shrimp	Insignificant. Of small value.	Where in my life am I ready to feel more worthy?
Shrine *See also* Temple.	Sacred part of self.	What part of me is worthy? What do I worship in myself?
Shrinking	Inadequacy. Too small.	Where in my life—or by whom—do I feel diminished?
Sick	Work on healing or well-being.	What part of myself am I preparing to heal?
Sidewalk	Life's pathway.	How am I avoiding the mainstream of my life? Where in my life do I want to take my time?
Sideways	Indirect approach.	Where in my life do I wish to be more straightforward?

Silver	Precious. Flexible. Spiritual strength.	What part of my spirit needs strengthening?
Singing	Joyous celebration. Praise. Communication of feeling.	What do I want to celebrate or communicate?
Sink	Minor release or cleansing.	What incidental issues do I wish to wash away?
Sinking	Descent into unconscious.	How am I ready to get to the bottom of things?
Sister	Feminine self. Fellowship.	What do I admire or judge in myself?
Six *See also* Numbers.	Expansion. Organization. Harmony. Domesticity.	What am I ready to commit to?
Skateboard	Youthful expression of power. Joyous freedom of movement.	Where in my life do I seek rejuvenation?
Skating *See also* Ice.	Rapid movement with great ease. Grace.	What am I ready to move across with ease?
Skeleton *See also* Body parts; Bone.	Work on support or structure. Remains.	Where in my life do I feel disconnected or falling apart?

167

Image:	Associations:	Ask Yourself:
Skiing *See also* Snow.	High speed, active movement. Physical skill and balance.	What part of me is ready to enjoy greater freedom of movement?
Skin *See also* Body parts.	Surface of the self. Sensitivity. Connection between inner and outer.	What is on the surface?
Skirt *See also* Clothing.	Lower self. Passions.	What signals am I sending?
Skunk *See also* Animals, wild.	Passive aggression.	Where in my life do I feel the need to protect myself?
Sky	Limitless freedom. Expansion.	Where in my life can I be without limits?
Skyscraper	Lofty aspiration. Worldly goals.	What do I wish to achieve? How high am I ready to climb?
Slapping	Force of attention.	What do I wish or fear to draw attention to?
Slaughterhouse	Sacrificial death.	What part of me dies for the rest to survive?

Sledgehammer	Massive destruction.	What am I tearing down?
Sleeping	Unconscious. Deep relaxation and rest.	What part of me is ready to awaken?
Sleeping bag	Shelter. Warmth. Protection.	What part of the unconscious do I wish to safely explore?
Slime	Unclean emotions.	What feelings am I ready to clean up?
Slip *See also* Clothing.	Private or inner self.	What do I wish or fear to reveal to the world?
Slug	Lazy. Unevolved.	What wishes to take form in me?
Small *See* Little.		
Smell	Intuition based on senses.	What smells bad or good in this situation?
Smiling	Work on joy or sorrow.	What makes me happy? What am I longing for?
Smoking *or* smoke *See also* Cigarette.	Restricted vision. Residue. Screen.	What is hidden? What do I want to hide?

169

Image:	Associations:	Ask Yourself:
Smothered	Work on freedom and trust.	Where in my life am I preparing to express my strength?
Smuggling	Work on ownership or control.	What has been denied to me? What do I want to possess?
Snake *See also* Animals, wild.	Energy. The serpent power of kundalini. Sexuality.	What energy am I ready to express or understand?
Snow	Purity. Emotion in suspension. Clarity. Ends and beginnings.	What is over? Where in my life do I want a fresh start?
Soap	Cleansing. Purification.	Do I need to clean up my act?
Soldier	Work on confrontation.	What am I ready to challenge? Where in my life do I fear challenge?
Son	Youthful, masculine aspect of self.	Where in my life am I ready to express youthful power?
Sorrow	Work on grief. Sadness.	What old pain do I wish to heal?
South	Ease. Freedom from constraint. Relaxation.	What part of me seeks release?

Term	Meaning	Question
South America *or* South American	Spontaneity. Volatility. Conquest.	What conflict am I ready to master?
Spaceship *or* Space *See also* Outer space; Rocket.	Exploration of consciousness or inner realms. Transcendence of physical limitations.	What greater consciousness am I seeking or making contact with?
Spanking	Work on childish rage.	What part of me wants to grow up?
Speaking	Communication. Message.	What am I telling myself?
Spear *See also* Weapon.	Wounding projectile. Attack from a short distance.	What fears am I ready to look at more closely?
Speeding *See also* Vehicles.	Work on fulfillment.	What will I miss if I don't slow down?
Sphere *See* Circle.		
Sphinx	Mystery. Riddles.	What secrets do I seek to understand?
Spicy	Flavor. Intensity.	Where in my life do I seek more stimulation? What heightens my experience?

171

Image:	Associations:	Ask Yourself:
Spider	The dark feminine force. Spinner of webs. Patience. Organization.	Do I fear or admire these qualities in myself?
Spigot *See* Faucet.		
Spine *See also* Body parts.	Support. Responsibility.	What holds me up?
Spiral	Dynamic movement. Evolution. Cycles.	Where in my life am I growing and expanding?
Spire	Direction of aspirations. Highest goals.	What am I reaching towards? What inspires me?
Splinter	Minor pain or inconvenience.	What small discomfort am I ready to heal?
Sports	Playing the game. Honor.	What game am I playing?
Spring *See also* Water.	Source. Beginning.	Where in my life am I allowing my feelings new expression?
Spring (season)	Cycle of growth. Generation.	What am I incubating?
Spy	Work on secrecy.	Where in my life am I ready to open up?

Square
See also Four.
Stability. Matter. Strength. Sudden change.
What in my life is stable for me? Where is my stability about to change?

Squid
Wariness. Strangling.
Where in my life am I ready to be seen or to speak out?

Squirrel
See also Animals, wild.
Hoarding. Running in place.
Where in my life am I ready to feel more secure?

Stabbing
Fear of betrayal.
Where in my life am I ready to be more trusting?

Stadium
Arena. Exhibition.
What skill am I ready to perform?

Stage
Performance. Achievement.
What recognition do I crave or fear? What am I ready to show to the world?

Stagecoach
Adventurous journey.
In what ways do I seek excitement on my path?

Stairs
See also House.
Ascent. Going higher. Aspiration. Descent. Grounding.
What do I want to rise or descend to?

173

Image:	Associations:	Ask Yourself:
Stamp	Facility of communication.	What am I ready to say or hear?
Star	Source of light or illumination. Spiritual awakening.	Where in my life am I ready to shine forth?
Statue	Representation. Image.	What content do I wish to give form to?
Steak *See* Meat.		
Stealing *See* Theft.		
Steam	Power. Sometimes rage.	What feelings are heating up in me?
Stepfather *See also* Father.	Substitute authority or guidance.	What controls me? What do I care for?
Stepmother *See also* Mother.	Substitute nurturing or tending.	What do I approve of or disapprove of in myself?
Stepping-stones	Safe passage. Secure movement.	What method will get me there?

Stick	Natural tool or weapon. Potential.	What do I wish to make use of?
Stillborn	Failure to trust. Loss of innocence.	Where must I begin again?
Stink *See* Smell.		
Stomach *See also* Body parts.	Digestion of information or circumstances. Understanding.	What value can I receive from my experience?
Stone *See also* Rock.	Essence. Elemental self. Solidity.	What part of me is solid or impenetrable?
Store	Resources. Variety. Choice.	What new things am I seeking?
Storm	Tumultuous change.	What forces are struggling within me?
Stove	Warmth. Heat. Nourishment. Comfort.	What warms me? What is the source of my security or comfort?
Stranger	Unacknowledged aspect of self.	What part of my nature am I ready to know?
Strangling	Holding back communication.	What am I ready to say or hear?
Straw	Common. Fodder.	What is the true value of my simplicity? Where do I seek inner gold?

Image:	Associations:	Ask Yourself:
Stream *See also* Water.	The flow of feeling.	What feelings flow comfortably within me?
Street *See* Road.		
String	Joining. Restricting.	What do I wish to tie together? What is confining?
Stripes	Order. Organized effort.	What line am I willing or unwilling to follow?
Stroke	Resistance to change.	Where in my life am I ready to release control?
Stuffed animal *See* Toy animal.		
Stumble	Minor obstacles. Clumsiness.	How can I move more confidently along my life's path?
Stump	Interrupted or blocked growth.	Have I been growing in the wrong direction? Do I feel thwarted?

Submarine	Means of exploring unconscious or emotional states.	What feelings am I ready to examine?
Subway	Rapid movement through the unconscious.	What powerful drives can I make conscious use of?
Suffocation	Restriction. Self-doubt.	What part of me must expand for me to live?
Sugar	Sweetness. Indulgence. Sometimes forbidden pleasure.	What pleasures do I deny myself?
Suicide	Self-destruction. Giving up part of the self.	What part of me must go? What do I want to quit?
Suit *See also* Clothing.	Formality. Professional identity.	What power or ability do I wish to be recognized for?
Suitcase *See* Baggage; Luggage.		
Summer	Cycle of fruition. Fullness of growth.	What am I producing?
Summit *See also* Mountain; Peak.	Attainment. Goals.	What constitutes success for me?

Image:	Associations:	Ask Yourself:
Sun	Energy. Light. Source. Life-giving power.	What do I wish or fear to receive?
Sundress *See also* Clothing.	Comfortable exposure.	What pleasures am I seeking? What part of me is ready to relax?
Sunglasses	Protection. Glamour.	How do I wish to be seen? What vision must I protect myself from?
Sunrise	Awakening. Beginning. Hope.	Where in my life am I ready to start over?
Sunset	Rest. Completion of the cycle. Release.	What have I accomplished?
Surfing *See also* Water.	Riding the waves of feeling.	What powerful emotions am I ready to enjoy?
Surgery	Work on healing.	What part of me wants to be well?
Surrender	Work on yielding.	What old patterns or beliefs am I ready to part with?

Swamp *See also* Water.	Overwhelming, turgid feelings.	
Swelling	Out-of-control expansion.	What pressure am I ready to release?
Swimming *See also* Water.	Movement through feeling, often with feelings of accomplishment. Emotion as environment.	What emotional state is deeply satisfying to me? What emotional support do I seek?
Swimming pool *See also* Water.	The water of feeling contained by cultural constructs. Safety.	What feeling do I wish to contain safely?
Swimming underwater	Submersion in emotion.	What feelings am I submerged in?
Swimsuit *See also* Bathing suit.		
Sword *See also* Weapon.	Cutting away, especially the past or falsity.	What old ideas or beliefs am I prepared to sever?
Table	Place of activity.	What am I ready to examine or to do?
Talking	Communication.	What am I ready to express? To whom or what do I want to communicate?

179

Image:	Associations:	Ask Yourself:
Tan *See also* Colors.	Convention. Hard work. Propriety.	In what ways do I seek or avoid respectability?
Tank	Armor. Destructive protection. Mobile threat.	What is dangerous in my expression of power?
Tattoo	Unorthodox self-expression. Display.	What strange message am I ready to convey?
Tavern *See also* Bar.	Conviviality. Relaxation. Indulgence.	What fellowship do I thirst for?
Tea	Contentment. Companionship.	Where in my life am I ready to take my time?
Teacher	Learning. Discipline.	What do I want to know?
Teaching *See also* School.	Work on knowledge or communication.	Where in my life am I ready to acknowledge or share my wisdom?
Tear gas	Torturous feelings. Smothered by suffering.	What deep pain am I ready to wash away?
Teddy bear *See also* Toy animal.	Trust. Protection. Fetish of possession.	What must I trust in order to love and be loved?

Teenager
See Adolescent.

Teeth
See also Body parts.

Independence. Power. Ability to nourish and communicate.

Where in my life do I fear dependence? What do I wish to say?

Telephone

Communication at a distance.

To whom or to what do I want to reach out?

Telescope

Distant vision.

What do I want to observe more closely?

Television

Image or story about reality. Means of observing events.

What story am I creating? What do I want to observe?

Temple
See also Shrine.

Soul. Sanctuary.

What is the form of my inner peace?

Ten
See also Numbers.

New beginning on a higher octave. Groups.

What have I learned?

Tent
See also House.

Temporary house of the self.

What natural part of myself do I wish to reconnect with?

Terror
See also Fear.

Paralyzing fear. Loss of trust.

What is central to my well-being? What do I trust in myself?

181

Image:	Associations:	Ask Yourself:
Terrorist	Violence born of frustration.	Where in my life do I feel my power is thwarted?
Test	Ordeal or examination.	What abilities or knowledge am I ready to demonstrate?
Testicles *See also* Body parts.	Yang power. Masculinity.	What power am I ready to express?
Theft	Lack. Need. Judgment.	What do I fear I can't have or don't deserve? What am I afraid of losing?
Therapist	Work on self-acceptance and love.	What parts of myself are ready for integration?
Thigh *See also* Body parts.	Power of movement.	Am I strong enough to get where I want to go?
Thirty-three *See also* Numbers.	Salvation and temptation.	Where in my life have I succeeded or failed?
Thorn *See also* Splinter.	Prick of awareness.	What awakens me?
Thread	Frailty. Fragility.	What am I ready to strengthen?

Three *See also* Numbers; Triangle.	Trinity. Balance of opposites. Sociability.	How do I integrate my differences?
Throat *See also* Body parts.	Communication. Trust. Creativity.	What am I ready to hear and say?
Thugs	Ugly forms of power. Misuse of energy.	Where in my life am I ready to clean up my act? How is power threatening to me?
Ticket	Means of admission.	What new experience or destination am I heading for?
Tidal wave *See also* Water.	Overwhelming emotion.	What feelings are threatening to me?
Tiger *See also* Animals, wild.	Power. Wild beauty. Sexual force.	What is dangerous in me?
Tights *See also* Clothing.	Shaping. Firming.	What can I safely expose?
Time	Attachment. Organization.	Where in my life am I ready to be carefree?

183

Image:	Associations:	Ask Yourself:
Tires *See also* Vehicles.	Cushion. Shock absorption.	Where in my life do I need to smooth my way?
Toad *See also* Animals, wild.	Infectious ugliness.	How or why have I concealed my true beauty?
Toe *See also* Body parts.	Beginning, especially of movement.	Where am I preparing to go?
Toilet *See also* Bathroom; Excrement; Urinating.		
Tombstone	Memorial. Record.	How do I wish to be remembered? What do I leave behind?
Tongue *See also* Body parts.	The pleasure of taste.	What am I eager to try?
Tools	Work on productivity.	What do I want to do or create?
Top *See also* Above.	Culmination. Resolution. Perfection.	What point have I reached?

Term	Meaning	Question
Topless *See also* Breast.	Exposure. Invitation.	How do I exhibit love?
Tornado	Violent force of destruction.	What dramatic change can I see approaching?
Torture	Part of the self tormented by the rest.	How am I hard on myself?
Tower	Rise above. Ascendancy. Sometimes isolation.	What accomplishment do I seek or fear?
Toy animal	Playful relationship with the natural world. Freedom from responsibility.	Where do I want more pleasure in my life?
Toys	Youthful play. Practicing life's responsibilities.	In what way am I ready to enjoy my life more?
Tractor	Sturdiness. Resourcefulness.	What am I processing?
Traffic *See also* Vehicles.	Chaotic power or movement.	What prevents me from going where I want or need to go?
Traffic jam *See also* Vehicles.	Frustrated power or movement.	Where is my energy blocked?
Trailer *See also* Vehicles.	Following. Impediment.	What extra load do I carry?

Image:	Associations:	Ask Yourself:
Train *See also* Travel; Vehicles.	Movement made while observing the areas covered or traveled.	What do I wish to observe as I change my life?
Trance *See also* Channeling.	Altered state. Expanded consciousness.	What part of my inner self am I ready to explore?
Transplant	New life.	What part of me feels worn out? Where in my life do I seek renewal?
Travel *See also* Vehicles.	Movement from one way of life or attitude to another.	Where am I going? Where do I want to go?
Treasure	Fulfillment. Integration. Material or spiritual reward.	What do I need to feel complete?
Treaty *See also* Agreement.		
Tree *See also* Wood.	Natural process. Structure of life.	Where in my life am I ready to grow?
Trench	Hiding place. Concealment.	Where in my life do I need to feel safe? What do I want to hide?

186

Trial	Test. Resolution of conflict.	What is at issue?
Triangle *See also* Three.	Dynamic power. Integration of opposites.	Where in my life am I developing power by integrating internal opposition?
Tricycle *See also* Vehicles.	Immature power. Playful movement.	Am I mature enough to get there? Am I enjoying the journey?
Tropics	Torrid. Luxuriant.	What do I wish to indulge myself in?
Trousers *See also* Clothing.	Lower self. Passions.	What signals am I sending?
Truck *See also* Vehicles.	Ability to carry the load.	Can I handle the responsibility?
Trust fund	Security. Control.	How am I ready to take care of myself?
Trusting	Work on self-acceptance.	What part of myself am I ready to integrate?
Tumor	Protective growth.	What old pain am I ready to release?

187

Image:	Associations:	Ask Yourself:
Tunnel	Path through inner space. Ordeal.	What light leads me on?
Turd *See* Excrement.		
Turquoise *See also* Colors.	Healing. Good luck. Protection.	Where in my life do I feel safe?
Turtle *See also* Animals, wild.	Protection. Perseverance.	Where in my life do I feel safe when I take my time?
Twenty-two *See also* Numbers.	Earthly mission. Self and others.	What do I trust?
Twigs	Small growth.	Where in my life am I growing?
Twin	Work on identity. Mirror image.	What do I reflect?
Two *See also* Numbers.	Duality. Opposition. Balance. Partnership.	How do I relate?
UFO *See also* Alien.	Fear and joy of the unknown. Distant realms.	Where am I ready to expand into unknown realms?

Umbilical cord	Link between old and new self.	How am I connected with my emerging self?
Umbrella	Protection from emotional storms.	What is raining down on me?
Under	Unconscious. Lower aspect of self.	What am I ready to bring forth?
See also Bottom.		
Underground	Unconscious material.	What is ready to rise to consciousness?
Underpants		
See Clothing; Underwear.		
Underwater	Submersion in emotion.	What emotions am I submerged within?
See also Swimming; Water.		
Underwear	Private self. Sexual identity.	What are my hidden feelings?
See also Clothing.		
Undressing	Exposing true or inner self.	Who am I underneath it all?
Unfeeling	Work on denial of emotion.	Where in my life am I prepared to be less sensitive?
Unicorn	Purity. Magical consciousness. Union of divine and animal nature.	Where in my life am I ready to align my animal nature with my spiritual essence?

189

Image:	Associations:	Ask Yourself:
Uniform *See also* Clothing.	Conformity.	Where in my life do I wish to share with others or to break free of rules?
Universe *See* School.	Totality of being. Wholeness.	Where in my life do I feel complete?
University	Higher learning.	What knowledge do I wish to expand?
Upside down	Reversal. Confusion.	What do I want to straighten out?
Urinating *or* urine *See also* Bathroom.	Release, usually of emotion. Anger. Embarrassment at emotional release.	What feelings am I clearing? Am I pissed off?
Vaccination	Protective injection.	What am I afraid of catching?
Vacuum	Emptiness. Absence. Potential.	What is missing? What fills me?
Vacuum cleaner	Cleanliness. Order.	What do I want to be rid of? What am I cleaning up?
Vagina *See also* Body parts.	Female sexuality. Yin receptivity.	What do I receive? What receives me?

Valley	Protection. Safety. Ease.	What makes me comfortable?
Vampire	Energy-draining fear.	What pursues me? Where in my life do I deny my own power?
Van	Practical power. Convenience.	How do I share my power? How much or how many can I carry?
See also **Vehicles.**		
Vase	Receptivity. Display.	What am I ready to receive?
Vegetable	Healthy food. Natural sustenance.	What am I hungry for?
Vehicles	Power. Movement. What gets you there.	How powerful am I? How do I feel about power?
See also subheadings.		
—*bicycle*	Self-propulsion. Recreation.	Do I have enough strength to make it? Will it be fun?
—*boat*	Movement across the depths of feeling.	What emotions can I safely negotiate?
—*brakes*	Control or slowing of movement.	Where in my life am I ready to feel more secure with my power?
—*bus*	Shared journey. Mass transit.	How does my personal power relate to mass consciousness?

191

Image:	Associations:	Ask Yourself:
—car	Personal power. Ego.	Can I get there? Who am I?
—convertible	Glamourous power. Parade.	What power am I ready to display?
—helicopter	Movement in many directions.	Where in my life do I want more freedom of movement?
—hydrofoil	Soaring above the sea of feeling.	What emotions no longer inhibit me?
—jeep	Ruggedness. Utility. Efficiency.	Where in my life must I be sturdy to reach my goal?
—limousine	Luxurious power. Extravagance.	Where in my life am I ready to be conspicuous in my expression of power?
—motorcycle	Virility. Vigor. Display.	How hot am I? Where in my life am I ready to be more masterful?
—plane	Rapid movement across great distance.	Am I in a hurry for change?
—R.V.	The joy of power. Rugged amusement.	Where in my life am I ready to have more fun with my power?

—seat belt	Safety restraint.	What holds my power in check?
—speeding	Work on fulfillment.	What will I miss if I don't slow down?
—tires	Cushion. Shock absorption.	Where in my life do I need to smooth my way?
—traffic	Chaotic power or movement.	What prevents me from going where I want or need to go?
—traffic jam	Frustrated power or movement.	Where is my energy blocked?
—trailer	Following. Impediment.	What extra load do I carry?
—train	Movement made while observing the areas covered or traveled.	What do I wish to observe as I change my life?
—tricycle	Immature power. Playful movement.	Am I mature enough to get there? Am I enjoying the journey?
—truck	Ability to carry the load.	Can I take on the responsibility?
—van	Practical power. Convenience.	How do I share my power? How much or how many can I carry?

Image:	Associations:	Ask Yourself:
Veil See also Clothing.	Illusion. Mystery.	What do I want to hide or to reveal?
Velvet	Softness. Luxury.	What is too hard for me? Where in my life am I vulnerable?
Veteran	Survivor of conflict.	What battle is over for me?
Video games	High-tech competition. Skill. Dexterity.	What new abilities are available to me?
Violet See also Colors.	Spirituality. Boundary between visible and invisible realms. Aristocracy.	To what do I aspire?
Volcano	Eruption of unconscious or repressed material.	What must I clear?
Volunteer	Work on willingness.	What do I have to offer? What do I stand up for?
Vomit or vomiting	Throwing up indigestible thoughts or feelings.	What do I need to get rid of?
Voyeurism See also Sex.	Safe distance from desires.	What do I want or fear to be close to?

Vulture	Scavenger.	How am I nourished by the experience of my past?
Waiter or waitress	Work on service. Servility.	What service am I ready to provide? Where am I tired of serving?
Walking	Natural movement. Exercise.	Where am I going? Am I moving fast enough?
Wall See also House.	Barrier. Defense. Partition. Protection.	What am I ready to integrate? What separation is necessary for me? What is on the other side?
Walrus See also Animals, wild.	Massive sensitivity.	Where in my life am I ready to be less threatening?
War	Violence. Conflict.	What parts of me are in conflict?
Warehouse	Storage of resources.	What am I ready to put away or to unpack?
Warrior See also Soldier; Veteran; War.	Work on challenges.	What am I ready to dare or to confront?

Image:	Associations:	Ask Yourself:
Wart	Noxious growth. Ugliness.	Where in my life am I ready to be more attractive?
Wasp	Stinging anger.	Where in my life do I want to strike out?
Watch *See also* Clock; Time.	Limitation. Division.	Where in my life do I want to be carefree?
Water *See also subheadings;* Elements.	Emotion. Dissolving. Yielding. Fluid. Release. Cleansing.	What am I feeling?
—*bay*	Shelter. Enclosure.	Where do I feel calm?
—*creek*	The flow of feeling.	What feelings flow comfortably within me?
—*dew*	Gentle release of emotion.	What feelings can I safely express?
—*dripping*	Trickle of emotion.	What am I releasing, bit by bit?
—*faucet*	Control or release of emotion.	What feelings do I turn on and off?

—*flood*	Overflow of emotion.	What feelings are too much for me?
—*fountain*	Emotion springing forth. Freedom of emotional expression. Release.	What feelings are welling up in me?
—*frozen*	Preservation. Restraint.	What rigid feelings am I ready to dissolve?
—*harbor*	Shelter. Safety.	Where in my life do I find emotional peace?
—*hose*	Flexibility. Flow of emotion.	How well do I communicate my feelings?
—*ice*	A rigid feeling state. Frozen.	What feelings are locked within or ready to be melted away?
—*lake*	Contained emotion. Often a sense of tranquillity or peace.	What feelings do I comfortably contain?
—*melting*	Letting go.	What old structures am I ready to dissolve?
—*mist*	Delicate expanse of feeling. Cool and comfortable.	What emotional field surrounds me?

197

Image:	Associations:	Ask Yourself:
—*mud*	Messy feelings. Fertility. Stuck.	What emotions am I ready to clean up?
—*ocean*	Vast, limitless feeling. Sometimes an overwhelming emotion. Rich with abundant life.	What part of me relates to such vastness?
—*puddle*	Small but messy emotions.	What minor discomfort am I feeling?
—*rain*	Release of emotion. May be gentle and nourishing or dramatically threatening.	What feelings are pouring down on me?
—*rapids*	Active, stimulating emotions.	How comfortable am I with intense feelings?
—*reef*	Danger or safety of hidden emotions.	What underlies my feelings?
—*river*	Flowing and active. May include dangerous rapids; may be smooth and tranquil.	What feelings are actively moving within me?
—*sea* See Water: *ocean.*		
—*spring*	Source. Beginning.	Where in my life am I allowing my feelings new expression?

—stream
See Water: *creek.*

—swamp   Overwhelming, turgid feelings.   What old emotional patterns are beginning to change for me?

—swimming pool   The water of feeling contained by cultural constructs. Safety.   What feeling do I wish to safely contain?

—tidal wave   Overwhelming emotion.   What feelings are threatening to me?

—waterfall   Dramatic going with the flow. May be frightening or powerfully releasing.   Where in my life am I ready to take the plunge?

—waterfront   Dangerous or untrustworthy feelings.   What emotions are threatening to me?

—well   Source. Shared resources.   What feelings am I ready to share?

—wet suit   Safety and comfort in the realm of feeling.   What depths of emotion do I want to safely explore?

Waterfront
See also Water.   Dangerous or untrustworthy feelings.   What emotions are threatening to me?

199

Image:	Associations:	Ask Yourself:
Weapon	Work on expression of energy. Offense and defense. Aggression.	Where in my life am I ready to be more open and receptive?
Weaving	Fabrication. Intimacy.	What am I putting together?
Web *See also* Spider.	Communication. Network. Skill. Trap.	What do I wish to control or to understand? What holds me back?
Wedding *See also* Marriage.	Celebration of union.	What do I joyously unite with?
Weed	Rugged fertility. Undesired growth.	What am I cultivating?
Well *See also* Water.	Source. Shared resources.	What feelings am I ready to share?
Weeping *See also* Crying.		
Weight lifting	Strength developed through effort. Making light of burdens.	How do my responsibilities make me strong?
Werewolf	Monstrous instincts.	What part of me is overcivilized? Where in my life are my instincts repressed?

West	Ending. Death. Return to beginning.	Where am I heading?
Wet suit *See also* Water.	Safety and comfort in the realm of feeling.	What depths of emotion do I want to safely explore?
Whale *See also* Animals, wild.	Power of the unconscious. Truth and strength of inner being.	What great truth am I ready to accept?
Wheel	Repetition. Totality.	What moves me to completion?
White *See also* Colors.	Purity. Clarity. Coldness.	What do I seek to purify?
Whore *See* Prostitute.		
Widow *or* widower	Solitude. Isolation.	What part of me is lonely?
Wife	Yin aspect of self. Partner.	What have I joined with?
Wind *or* windy	Stimulation. Sensory overload.	Where in my life do I seek stimulation? Where do I feel overwhelmed?
Windmill *See also* Wind.	Power of movement. Stimulating force.	What powerful thoughts are stirring within me?

201

Image:	Associations:	Ask Yourself:
Window *See also* House.	Vision. Seeing and being seen.	What am I willing to see? What do I wish to reveal or conceal?
Wine *See also* Alcohol; Drunk.	Conviviality. Celebration.	What do I wish to enjoy?
Wing	Flight. Freedom. Transcendence.	What am I ready to rise above?
Winter	Cycle of disintegration. Rest. Rebirth.	What am I preparing to bring forth?
Witch	Negative feminine. Black magic. If positive, intuition and natural wisdom.	What feminine power do I hold or fear?
Wizard	Work on skill or sorcery.	What powers do I seek to master?
Wolf *See also* Animals, wild.	Instinct. Appetite. Threat. Loyalty.	What instincts are a threat to me? What are my instinctive loyalties?
Woman	Feminine aspect. Receptivity.	Where in my life am I ready to be more receptive?

Wood *See also* Lumber; Tree.	Growth.	What is my natural form?
Woods *See* Forest.		
Working *See* Employment; Job.		
Workshop	Process. Self-understanding.	What skills do I wish to develop?
Worm	Decay. Insignificance.	Where in my life am I ready to assert myself?
Wound *or* wounded	Site of grief or anguish.	What damage am I ready to heal?
Wreck	Violent destruction. Barrier to progress.	What or who wants to stop me?
Wrestling	Work on strength and stamina.	What am I struggling to understand or control?
Writing	Self-expression. Record of experience.	What do I wish to put on record?
X ray	Seeing inside. Dangerous energies.	What lies within? What do I fear if I penetrate the surface image?

Image:	Associations:	Ask Yourself:
Yard *See also* Garden; Grass.	Enclosure. Personal space.	What surrounds me?
Yarn	Binding. Patterns.	What am I connecting or creating?
Yelling	Emotional release.	What must I forcefully express?
Yellow *See also* Colors.	Vitality. Intellect. Clarity.	What do I wish to understand?
Yeti *See also* Animals, wild.	Man-beast. Legendary.	What part of my greater self is stalking me?
Young *or* youth	Immaturity. Vitality.	What part of me is blossoming?
Zodiac	Archetypes. Aspects of consciousness.	How do I relate to my own divine nature?
Zombie	Living death.	What am I afraid to let go of?
Zoo *See also* Animals, wild.	Wildness under control.	What instincts do I want to observe or enjoy in safety?

Appendix
Additional Resources for Rewarding Dream Work

Beyond Your Wildest Dreams: Dream Incubation Tapes, Series I and II

Dream incubation tapes offer you an efficient, convenient means of intensifying and directing your dreams. You should use them at night, preferably with headphones, as you are falling to sleep.

Each tape begins with a guided meditation that relaxes your body and clears your mind, producing a body-relaxed, alert-mind state similar to the state associated with various systems of meditation. The tapes then guide you to create intense images and visions that will lead to stimulating and memorable dreams.

The original music accompanying the tapes was produced for the series by the internationally acclaimed composer Deuter.

Following is a description of each of the tapes in Series I and II.

Series I

Tape 1

Side One: Dream Clearing. If you are interested in beginning a program of conscious dreaming, I recommend you start with this tape, which was created specifically to help you remove old dream material. Old images, and particularly recurrent dream patterns that may have been blocking your dream memory for years, will be processed and washed from your consciousness. Listen to "Dream Clearing" for a few nights before you turn the cassette over to Side Two and begin enjoying the delicious, sensuously rich dream experiences that the "Dream Recall" side often produces.

Side Two: Dream Recall. This tape stimulates each sense with vivid images. The result is intense dream imagery and better recall of it.

Tape 2

Side One: Dream Guidance. This tape leads to a dream meeting with the aspect of yourself that can guide you comfortably and securely into knowledge of your own future.

Side Two: Dream Healing. Through guided imagery, you visit Epidauros—healing center of the ancient world—to receive dreams that stimulate healing on an inner level.

Tape 3

Side One: Dream Exploration. Fly into dream adventures and explore other realms of consciousness while your body sleeps safely and comfortably.

Side Two: The Black Velvet Room. This tape opens a dream world of sensuous pleasure and deep, refreshing sleep—an antidote to even the most stressful waking life. A number of clients have reported to me that this tape is an effective antidote for insomnia.

Series II

Tape 1

Side One: Dreamsex. Explore the depths of your own sexuality in the privacy and safety of the dream state. Opening the dream door to sexual fulfillment often leads to greater creative vitality in your waking life.

Side Two: The Corridor of Dreams. This tape encourages dreams that offer specific information about your future projects—including their most likely outcome and barriers to their success.

Tape 2

Side One: Dreamlover. This tape leads to a meeting in the dream state with your ideal other. You may meet an aspect of yourself, ready for integration, or actual future lovers, who

207

invite you to approach them and complete the union so deeply desired.

Side Two: The Dark Vessel. This tape uses the classic imagery of setting out in a small boat across an expanse of dark water. I originally created it to lead the dreamer to "the other side" — to dream contact with friends and relatives who are dead. It has also provided a valuable tool for terminally ill clients who want to explore the after-death state in their dreams, prior to their own death.

Because of the power of the imagery, "The Dark Vessel" also helps you investigate and release old fears, whether these fears concern the subject of death or are related to other core issues. Several clients have found it worked well to alternate this tape with the "Dream Healing" tape (Series I, Tape 2, Side Two) or with the "Dream Clearing" tape (Series I, Tape 1, Side One).

I continue to use all of the tapes regularly, although I do have personal favorites and often choose "Dream Recall" (Series I, Tape 1, Side Two) simply because I love having all of my senses active in dreams — tasting dream food, smelling dream flowers, being acutely aware of colors and the texture of things.

Order Form: Beyond Your Wildest Dreams:
Dream Incubation Tapes, Series I and II

All prices include postage and handling. For delivery outside the U.S., please add an additional $2 per order.

Please send me:

Series #	Item description:	Price each	Total cost
Series I	All three tapes of Series I	$28.50	$_____
Series I	Dream Clearing/Dream Recall	$12.00	_____
Series I	Dream Guidance/Dream Healing	$12.00	_____
Series I	Dream Exploration/ Black Velvet Room	$12.00	_____
Series II	Both tapes of Series II	$22.50	_____
Series II	Dreamsex/Corridor of Dreams	$12.00	_____
Series II	Dreamlover/Dark Vessel (after-death state)	$12.00	_____

Enclosed payment of: $_____

Make check or money order payable to:
Real Dreams, 53–086 Halai Rd., Hau'ula, HI 96717

Method of payment: ___ check ___ money order
___ Visa ___ Mastercard

Credit Card Account Number: Expiration: Month Year

_____ ___ ___

Credit card orders must include a signature.

Signature: _____ Date: _____

Name: _____ (please print)

Address: _____

City: _____ State: _____ Zip: _____

Mail to: Real Dreams, 53–086 Halai Road, Hau'ula, HI 96717

To Contact the Author

Alice Anne Parker conducts residential dream workshops and Reiki healing intensives at her home, a former Tibetan Buddhist retreat center on the windward side of the island of O'ahu, Hawaii.

If you would like information and a schedule of upcoming workshops, please write to her at: Buddha-Buddha, 53–086 Halai road, Hau'ula, HI 96717. Please include a stamped, self-addressed envelope for reply.

Here is a Tantalizing Preview of Alice Anne Parker's
New Metaphysical Adventure Novel

The Last of the Dream People

"In this wonderful book, Alice Anne Parker establishes herself as a magnificent storyteller and spiritual teacher. I was unable to put it down."
   —Michael Peter Langevin, Co-publisher, *Magical Blend* magazine

"Kilton Stewart meets *The Kin of Ata.*"
   —Robert Moss, Author of *Conscious Dreaming* and *Dreamgates*

❧ 1 ☙

Paper Doll was going down. Dense smoke filled the cockpit. I fought a losing battle with the wheel. "Keep 'er nose up, Kilty." Rusty Cable's voice was in my ear. "Keep 'er nose up." I glanced over at my copilot. His head pitched forward at an impossible angle, left arm hanging uselessly at his side. Then he seemed to raise his head, grinning his cocky grin at me, his freckled face cherubic. He was a happy-go-lucky Van Johnson to my somber Greg Peck. We'd flown together since the beginning. "Got to keep 'er nose up a little longer." I returned to my endless chore, fighting against the ever-increasing force pulling us down, down out of the sky. Fighting my increasing exhaustion.

God only knows where we are. Dense, black, steaming jungle below. We were more than halfway into the run when the ack-ack hit. Little puffs of white smoke far below. It was only a milk run anyway. We didn't expect any action. Didn't even have an escort. Hadn't seen a Nip on this side of the mountains for days. Then we took the hit.

I sent the navigator back to check the damage. He hadn't returned to the cockpit when they hit us again. *What is down there, for Christ's sake?* The radio was out. Must have gone with the first attack. But someone in the squadron must've seen us turn. Thought we could make it back. Then the second antiaircraft attack ripped through our belly. I turned off course.

Got to find a place to put her down. Can't risk those trees. God, I'm too tired. I can't make it, Rusty. This time he doesn't reply, even in my fevered imagination. A dark, sweetish stench fills the cabin, mixing with the ominous smell of burning insulation. *Holy cow, Rusty, did you crap your pants?*

God, I don't want to die! Not on a milk run, for Christ's sake. This milk wagon is filled with five tons of high-quality explosive and detonating caps that go off if somebody farts loud enough. Too heavy a load. Should only carry four. Too much fuel left in the tanks. Too much high octane fuel to take her down safely.

I risk dropping a hand down to rest for a second on my leg. Something's wrong there, but maybe I don't want to know about it. I'm reassured. My hand feels a leg, and even better, leg feels hand. The nose dips. I drag it back up with both arms, pulling like they're coming out of shoulder sockets. *I can't do it alone. Rusty?*

I must be hallucinating. Some part of me knows he'll never answer again. Still I see him raise his head and look meaningfully in front of the nose. I follow his gaze. Directly ahead of us looms a massive butte, its crown covered with dense, dark green growth, behind it an even higher mountain reaching towards the clouds. I can't get the nose up. We'll never make it over. Then I hear Rusty's voice again. "Take her down now. You can do it, Kilty. Just let her float down. Like a leaf. Take her down easy, real, real easy."

I look where he seems to point. At the foot of the butte, on the left side, a clearing. Too small. Maybe a little longer than a couple of football fields. Way too small. I need close to four thousand feet to put this baby down safely. *Paper Doll* is no slim beauty. She's a deep-bosomed babe loaded with TNT. Maybe I can drop into the slot and coast into the jungle growth at the end. Let the jungle absorb the impact. No choice anyway. Starting to drop now. Slow her down as much as possible. Not enough control. Mustn't stall and drop too soon. Nose up again. Too tired. Treetops whipping at the undercarriage. Keep the nose up. Fighting against gravity. Fighting the pain.

We drop into the hole and only seconds later impact the green wall at the end of the line.

It's completely dark. I seem to be tied up. Can't move. Can't see. Hot. Burning up. A trickle of cool water in my mouth. There is a fragrance. It is here. Then gone. Pain claims me.

I am awake. Pretending to be asleep. I still can't see. My eyes are covered by something cool. Left arm and shoulder immobile. Right moves a little. Fingers can flex. I feel naked. Still burning. Fingers feel something like a latticework or irregular net wrapped around my torso. Some Jap torture device? It's completely rigid. Yields only slightly when I inflate my lungs to press against it. Hurts to breathe. Ribs broken. I think the thing runs all the way down my left leg. Why can't I raise my right hand? Any movement produces excruciating pain. Dry, sweet smell. Sandalwood. Something tickles a distant memory. I drift off.

I remember sitting in a red booth at a Chinese restaurant on a narrow side street in Seattle, down by the docks. I'm a little kid. Dragons swirl on columns holding up the ceiling. Incense, sandalwood incense. The waiter has a queue. He brings me a few ugly dried-up things arranged on a small red lacquer plate. Gestures that I should put one in my mouth. I'm a bit suspicious, but I pop one in. It is dry, dense, but then I bite into it, releasing a piercing, perfumy juice.

I am given more of them to take home in a rough brown cardboard box. We're driving back to Eugene tonight. My folks are in the front seat of Blackie, our Ford coupe. I fit perfectly on the shelf under the back window. I have a blanket and a pillow. The stars fill the window above me, crisp against the winter sky. The reassuring murmur of voices, my mom and dad speaking softly together. I pop another lichee in my mouth.

The next time I wake up I feel light through my eyelids. I still can't open my eyes. Still pain. Something cool is laid across the lids again. Smells green. The fragrance is present. I am touched very gently here and there by something. A sense of great delicacy. A Chinese nurse? Japs don't have nurses for prisoners of war. Maybe they have other plans for me. Not torture. God, I hope not torture. Maybe they plan to save me for some triumphant public beheading. That's been popular lately. The heads of our men left on stakes for us to find when we take the villages. Medals and dog tags arranged underneath so we can identify the victims. I begin to shudder uncontrollably.

When I wake up again I smell, then feel, the presence of someone. Without thinking I turn my head towards the presence. A very small hand touches me gently on the palm of my right hand. It feels delicate, thin and papery. Then the voice. Dry, whispery. An accent. Asian, but with a slightly British inflection? A trick? Japs are tricky characters. *Be careful. Don't give too much away.*

"Welcome, Captain. I am not reading well, and your papers were singed. You are Captain Ste-ew-art, Keeltee, yes?" The "Stewart" was drawn out into several syllables. "You recover very nice, I think. Not to open eyes yet, please. Eyes okay, I am thinking, but not good yet. There is much pain yet, burns, yes, ribs, right leg, arm bones maybe broken, but good. Good, yes."

I'm not answering. Not yet. I've got to have a plan. I'll pretend ignorance. I'll be grateful for the rescue. Find out as much as I can first. My men? Could any have survived? Where are they? Other huts near here? Need to recover enough to make it through the jungle to our lines. Where the hell are we? How did that character know my nickname? That's not on any of my papers. Find out as much as possible first. Get well. Time to plan an escape. The presence is waiting.

"Drink now, Captain Keeltee. Good drink. You will sleep and dream most important dreams now. Have dreams now. I come back and you will tell me your good dreams, yes? We have waited long, longtime for you."

Something cool and slightly acrid is dripped into my mouth...

DIET FOR A NEW AMERICA
How Your Food Choices Affect Your Health, Happiness, and the Future of Life on Earth
by John Robbins
In this new edition of the classic that awakened the conscience of a nation, John Robbins brilliantly documents that our food choices can provide us with ways to enjoy life to the fullest, while making it possible that life itself might continue.

BEYOND FEAR
Twelve Spiritual Keys to Racial Healing
by Aeeshah Ababio-Clottey and Kokomon Clottey
Teaching that racial healing comes about through personal transformation, *Beyond Fear* offers readers twelve spiritual keys with which to explore their beliefs and feelings about racism.

WAY OF THE PEACEFUL WARRIOR
A Book That Changes Lives
by Dan Millman
A spiritual classic! The international best-seller that speaks directly to the universal quest for happiness.

FULL ESTEEM AHEAD
100 Ways to Build Self-Esteem in Children and Adults
by Diane Loomans with Julia Loomans
"*Full Esteem Ahead* is the best book on parenting and self-esteem that I know."—Jack Canfield, author of *Chicken Soup for the Soul*

HEALING YOURSELF WITH LIGHT
How to Connect With the Angelic Healers
by LaUna Huffines
The complete guide to the healing power of light for physical, mental, and emotional health.

For a complete catalog of H J Kramer titles,
please send your name and address to:
H J Kramer, P.O. Box 1082, Tiburon, CA 94920